Time Managemen

A Guidebook to Help You Manage Your Time and Get Things Done

Jason James, David Donaldson, Joe Allen

PUBLISHED BY:
Jason James
Copyright © 2012

Table of Contents

Chapter 1: The essentials of time management

"Your time is limited, so don't waste it living someone else's life and don't let the noise of others' opinions drown out your own inner voice. Most important, have the courage to follow your heart and intuition. They somehow already know what you truly want to become." – Steve Jobs

Do you ever ask yourself "where has the time gone?" and wonder why you are always scrambling to finish things at the last possible moment? Do you find it hard to find time to spend with your family and friends after work? Do you struggle to find time for rest and relaxation? You aren't the only one!

There are only 24 hours in a day. That is a non-negotiable. So how do we use that time? Well, the average person spends 8.5 hours sleeping, 1 hour on personal care and grooming, 2.5 hours on housework, 8.5 hours on work or school activities, and 3 hours caring for, or spending time with others. That adds up to 23.5 hours a day, leaving half an hour left for leisure, rest, and relaxation. Not much wiggle room there. That is unless you make every minute count and develop some great time management skills.

Although there are those for whom time management comes naturally, many people have difficulty with making sure they have everything done and are where they say they are going to be when they say they are going to be there.   It sounds easy enough to get tasks completed and get to appointments on time, but these are skills not easily applied for many people.   There are always things that get in the way of accomplishing tasks in a timely manner.   These can include a social life, family, school or work commitments.   It can become overwhelming to complete work tasks and still find time for baseball games, drinks with friends, dates, and family dinners.   Sometimes it's just difficult to calculate how long it will take to accomplish a task or get to an appointment.   If you judge that a meeting will take 30 minutes and it takes 60, the next task on the agenda gets pushed forward, and the slippery slope continues from there.   Learning to more accurately judge time is critical to improving time management. We know unexpected things come up and some days may not go as smoothly as we had expected or hoped.   That said- there are many things we can do to improve time management skills and make sure that on most days, tasks are accomplished with minimal stress.

What is time management

"Imagine there *is a bank that credits your account each morning with $86,400. It carries over no balance from day to day. Every evening the bank deletes whatever part of the balance you failed to use during the day. What would you do? Draw out every cent, of course! Each of us has such a bank. Its name is TIME. Every morning, it credits you with 86,400 seconds. Every night it writes off, as lost, whatever of this you have failed to invest to good purpose. It carries over no balance. It allows no overdraft. Each day it opens a new account for you. Each night it burns the remains of the day. If you fail to use the day's deposits, the loss is yours. There is no going back. There is no drawing against the "tomorrow." You must live in the present on today's deposits. Invest it so as to get from it the utmost in health, happiness, and success! The clock is running. Make the most of today. To realize the value of ONE YEAR, ask a student who failed a grade. To realize the value of ONE MONTH, ask a mother who gave birth to a premature baby. To realize the value of ONE WEEK, ask the editor of a weekly newspaper. To realize the value of ONE HOUR, ask the lovers who are waiting to meet. To realize the value of ONE MINUTE, ask a person who missed the train. To realize the value of ONE-SECOND, ask*

a person who just avoided an accident. Treasure every moment that you have! And treasure it more because you shared it with someone special, special enough to spend your time. Remember that time waits for no one. Yesterday is history. Tomorrow is mystery. Today is a gift. That's why it's called the present!" <u>*www.parablesite.com*</u>

Time management, according to Wikipedia, is *"the act or process of planning and exercising conscious control over the amount of time spent on specific activities, especially to increase effectiveness, efficiency or productivity"*. It refers to the steps that we take in order to schedule, plan and then carry out that plan in order to accomplish our various goals and activities. This careful scheduling and planning improves effectiveness and productivity in our daily lives. Time management involves setting goals, protecting time, prioritizing, and avoiding procrastination among many other things. It its most simple form, time management involves two steps:

A. **Decide what to do**
B. **Do it**

Am I a poor manager of time?

Before reading on consider the following list. If several of these traits or descriptors apply to you it is a signal that you would likely benefit from improving your time management skills.

- You are frequently behind schedule
- You have trouble finding things
- People assume you are going to be late
- You forget important tasks
- You do not have an updated calendar
- You double-book appointments

- You show up to an event at the wrong place or time
- Events and deadlines have a way of sneaking up on you
- Your e-mail inbox has many unread messages
- You frequently find yourself needing to reschedule appointments
- You are a procrastinator
- You have difficulty locating important phone numbers and addresses
- When you arrive at work you realize you have left needed items at home
- You do not delegate
- You do not say "no"
- Your bills are frequently paid late
- Others would describe you as being unreliable
- You don't have time for leisure or hobbies
- You are always rushing
- You are stressed

Is time management important to everyone?

Different countries have different ways of perceiving time and how it should be spent. Cultures can vary as to whether they have a short- or long-term focus on time, sequential versus simultaneous focus, or a past versus present orientation. Some countries, such as those in Northern Europe, think of time in more of a sequential way. This can be referred to as having a sequential focus or monochronic view of time. With this approach, one task is completed prior to starting on the next activity. We see this view frequently in the United States as well as Northern Europe.

In these places time is viewed as a concrete entity that should be carefully scheduled, protected, and managed.

Other cultures are synchronically organized, also referred to as polychromic time. This means that several tasks are carried out simultaneously. People from places such as the Middle East or Latin America share this view of time and think of it as more fluid and place less emphasis on schedules and arriving promptly for appointments. In Asian, Arab, and Southern European countries, high importance is placed on the establishment of positive relationships and less importance is placed on time keeping and productivity.

A culture that relies on a past orientation believes that knowledge of the past will guide the future. For these cultures, having a deep understanding of past patterns is essential. A present orientation reflects a focus on the current moment, without much reflection to the past or future. A future oriented culture is focused on constant improvement, achievement, and progression. These different viewpoints have a definite impact on the expectations for time management within a culture.

What are some of the most important theories and approaches to time management?

Much research has been done over the past hundred or more years that have had a direct reflection on our perception of effective time management. These come from business oriented as well as psychological points of view. It is worth reviewing these to determine if one strike a chord and can help guide you to choose strategies that will help you to improve your efficiency.

Maslow's hierarchy of needs

The first theory comes from a psychological and developmental viewpoint. Abraham Maslow wrote a "hierarchy of needs" in 1943 as part of his paper "*A Theory of Human Motivation*". This has become an important tool relating to how our internal state is impacted by our ability to manage time. It is frequently represented as a pyramid.

The base of the pyramid relates to a person's physiological needs. This level includes the things we need to have in order to survive: food, water, sleep, and air; the absolute basics and essentials. In order to have higher needs met, these needs must be met first. Recall how you feel when you are hungry. Are you at your most productive? Are you able to think deeply and flexibly? Most of us cannot which is why these essentials are reflected as a base for all other needs.

The next level of the pyramid reflects our need for safety and security. These are the things that made us feel healthy, secure and comfortable. This level might include having a comfortable and safe home, a secure job, a healthy body, and financial stability. Not having these things frequently puts people in a state of stress, making it difficult to focus on other things no matter how much we may try. When we do not feel safe and healthy, we frequently lose focus and are interrupted by our own worrying thoughts.

The next step targets our social needs, also referred to as our need for love and belonging. Having fulfilling relationships with others allows us to move up the hierarchy and become even more successful. Without them, many people experience depression, loneliness, and anxiety.

Moving up we have esteem needs. These needs refer to the qualities within us that allow us to feel good about ourselves and our skills. It also reflects our desire to be accepted and valued by others. Specific aspects of this level include our reputation, self-esteem, recognition, and achievements. At the top of the pyramid is self-actualization. People who reach their full potential in life have become self-actualized.

Brain hemisphere dominance

Other researchers focus on hemispheric thinking when referring to time management approaches. First, you would decide if you are a right brain or a left brain thinker. People who have a dominant left hemisphere tend to be:

- Logical
- Sequential
- Rational
- Analytical
- Objective
- Look at parts

Left brainers appreciate an orderly approach to tasks and become overwhelmed by chaos. They are planners and appreciate knowing the end result before determining the steps to get there. People with a left hemisphere dominance tend to complete tasks completely and do not generally wait until the last minute to do it. Left brain thinkers tend to be rule-followers and enjoy using traditional methods to schedule their time.

People who have a dominant right hemisphere tend to be:

- Random
- Intuitive
- Holistic
- Synthesizing
- Subjective
- Look at wholes

Right brainers appreciate a bit of disorganization and chaos. They tend to attack a project with gusto but may not persist and complete it as they are easily distracted while in the middle of a task. A person who is right brain dominant is not likely to appreciate being asked to schedule details and organize. Right brain thinkers find traditional methods of time management, rules, and systems limiting.

Time management styles

The most effective time management approach you can take is one that suits your personal style. In a paper published by The Columbus Citywide Training and Development Center, they present several approaches to time management.

The first approach is traditional time management. This system takes a structured approach to plan, prioritize, schedule and execute tasks. People who prefer this traditional method are typically organized, precise, structured, and have a preference for routines. This group of people is referred to in the Columbus paper as Analyticals.

Not everybody shares a love for that traditional approach. For these people, nontraditional time management techniques have been divided into three styles:

- Amiables- People for whom interactions with others is a priority. Their time is managed though these interactions

- Drivers- People with a tendency to respond to immediate needs by being flexible, resourceful, and practical

- Expressives- People who can plan strategies and solutions, manage concepts and ideas, and excel at complex projects and tasks.

People who prefer an amiable style tend to:

- see possibilities
- be empathetic and compassionate
- strive to find a deeper meaning
- see potential in others
- enjoy and seek out contact with others
- Communicate positively with others
- endeavor to help others through their work

People who prefer a driver's style tend to:

- enjoy being a part of the action
- be flexible
- be poor decision makers
- be risk takers
- excel at projects that are completed over a short time period
- be spontaneous
- be good at troubleshooting and crisis management
- be resourceful
- be rule breakers
- be practical

People who prefer an expressive style tend to:

- enjoy new ideas and concepts
- enjoy solving complex problems
- do not always follow-through
- Take a holistic approach to problem solving
- be unaware of other's feelings
- do well with complex projects
- have little tolerance for incompetence
- question
- challenge authority
- make great strategic planners

PIE approach to time management

PIE is a 3-step approach to time management. This is a fairly traditional strategy. P stands for "prepare a calendar". Do this by choosing a calendar or personal organizer and fill it with all scheduled appointments and due dates. The "I" stands for "implementing a weekly schedule". At the beginning of the week, create a list in your calendar or organizer containing all of the tasks you need to accomplish for the week. Estimate the amount of time you need to complete major tasks. Refer to your calendar daily to complete tasks as scheduled. "E" stands for "evaluate your daily schedule". To complete this step, prioritize the next day's tasks and ensure that the schedule is realistic.

Four Element Approach

This approach may seem out to be pretty far out there for many however, it is worth exploring. Eric Garner presents this approach in his article "Time Management: A New Approach from Ancient Greece". It is based on the ancient Greek theory of the Four Elements. The Greeks believed that all matter in the universe was made up solely of earth, fire, air, and water. Garner has applied these 4 elements in a symbolic way to approach time management.

Earth tasks are those which are completed in order to nourish and keep our bodies healthy and comfortable. It is the most basic of elements and ensures our continued existence. Specific earth tasks include sleeping, eating, and elimination. Earth tasks should take up about ¼ of the day. Fire tasks represent the "creative spark" within us. These tasks involve creating new ideas, taking risks, trying something new, and inventing. These activities are spontaneous, inspired, productive work. Fire tasks should take up about ¼ of the day. Air tasks involve thinking. These activities include goal-setting, planning, decision-making, and learning. These tasks involve turning on our thoughts and turning off physical activity. Air tasks take up about ¼ of the day. Water tasks are completed when we are with others. They represent our interactions and relationships with others. Water tasks should take up about ¼ of the day. In order to be most healthy and productive, Garner suggests that air tasks be followed by physical earth tasks, followed with creative fire work, followed by time with others (water work)

Now that you have all this information you will be able to apply principles from the theories outlined above to the strategies and tips outlined in the remainder of this report to improve your time management skills.

Chapter 2: Benefits of good time management and the consequences of poor time management

Many people find themselves frustrated by an inability to manage time in a way that allows him or her to be highly efficient and productive. In this chapter we will take a look at general reasons as to why people may have difficulty in this area. We will also look at the benefits and consequences of being more efficient with time.

Why am I having difficulty with time management?

The first step at improving skills in this area is to identify exactly where the problem is. Difficulties usually stem from one, or a combination of, of three general factors.

The first factor is poor time management due to repeated technical errors. This type of time mismanagement can be fixed by altering factors such as when high priority tasks are completed, how the amount of time it will take to complete a task is estimated, or how a person responds when the phone rings while he or she is engaged in another task.

The second factor is the presence of undesirable or inefficient external realities. This refers to environments with lots of distractions, unrealistic schedules, or that require too many commitments to too many people.

The last factor is psychological obstacles. There are several thought processes that impede productivity. These can include fear of failure, fear of success or resistance to change.

Consequences of poor time management

Poor time management can have a marked effect on physical health. Feeling like we aren't accomplishing all the things that we feel are necessary causes us to feel stressed. Stress is something that can have a negative impact on every facet of our lives, including our health, and should be taken very seriously. Studies have shown that people with high amounts of stress experience:

- difficulty sleeping
- upset stomach
- difficulty swallowing
- restlessness
- muscle tension
- increased heart rate
- decreased libido

If we are not sleeping or physically feeling well, our basic needs cannot be met and thus we are prevented from reaching our fullest potential. Stress also affects our mood and thinking in many ways including:

- irritability
- nervousness
- lack of energy

- mental slowness
- negative attitude
- anxiety
- forgetfulness
- frustration
- decreased amount of time spent with family and friends
- limited amount of time spent in relaxing activities

If we do not manage our time at work effectively there are many negative consequences including:

- Lack of achievement of assigned tasks
- wasted time
- missed deadlines
- poor work quality
- frequent mistakes
- poor focus
- decreased energy
- more internal interruptions
- decreased creativity
- impaired judgment

Benefits of good time management

The clearest benefit of improved time management is getting more done in less time. Take some time and think about all the things you would do with more time in your day. Would you take some you time? Visit with friends? Go on a date? Spend extra time with your child? Time will be at your disposal. In this chapter, we will explore some benefits of time management that may not be quite as clear.

Let us go back to Maslow's Hierarchy of Needs for a bit to talk about the advantages of managing your time more effectively. The bottom of the pyramid as you may recall is physiological needs. If these needs are not met, for example by not finding enough time to grocery shop, you are immediately placed in a stressful mindset and prohibited from moving much further up the pyramid. I know that is an extreme example; however the next levels up, safety and love/belonging, is more realistically where many people may fall apart as a result of poor time management. At this point, if we are not able to effectively manage all that is on our plate, we may start feeling like we are losing control over our career, financial stability, and health. Our relationships with others suffer when we can't make time to devote to them. And the time is there- we just need to gain control, organize, and rein it in. Up even higher in the pyramid is esteem and self-actualization. If we can't achieve these higher levels we will feel even more out of control, lack self-esteem, lack confidence, and continue to seek out a feeling of achievement.

Think about the benefits of increased efficiency at work. Increased productivity is likely to be noticed by higher-ups which could result in a raise or a promotion. When we are acknowledged for our achievements we move up on Maslow's Hierarchy due to increased self-esteem, self-confidence, and achievements. People who are frequently late, do not meet deadlines or missing appointments come across as being unreliable. These people are often looked-over for advancement opportunities. By increasing efficiency at work it is likely you will not have to stay late at the office or bring work home. This makes more time for family, friends, and hobbies. Not only will this reduce stress but our relationships with others will benefit because we are able to spend more quality time and without stress, these interactions can be much more positive and up-beat.

By becoming more organized and effective we avoid burnout. Being burned-out leaves us feeling physically and emotionally weak. It occurs when a person can no longer deal with the high demands being placed on them. Because you feel so lousy, even if you do complete tasks you remain behind and cannot meet expectations. Burnout can have several causes including:

- Overwhelming workload
- Working without clear goals
- Feelings of helplessness, powerlessness, or lack of control
- Having unrealistic expectations
- Ethical conflicts
- Working without recognition or promotional opportunities

Symptoms of burnout are physical and emotional and include:

- Headaches
- Difficulty sleeping
- Stomach and intestinal problems
- Fatigue
- Muscle aches
- High blood pressure
- Weight loss or weight gain
- Frequent colds
- Frustration
- Depression

- Anger

- Negative attitude

- Depression

- Irritability

- Apathy

Avoid burnout by being organized in a way that you know exactly how much of a workload you currently have. This puts things into perspective and defines a path for continuance or delegating. Burnout can also be treated by saying "no". Consistently having ½ done projects also adds weight to the load you are carrying. Try to see things through until they are finished. Also, don't let other people steal your time. Set your limits and expectations and follow through with them. Defend it!

When we start managing time more effectively we experience a change in attitude from reactive to proactive. By accurately planning for your day or the completion of a project, you are prepared for trips and stumbles. Your proactive approach will have a contingency plan to overcome these bloopers more quickly. Without this level of efficiency, a reactive reaction has to take place. There is no plan and therefore valuable time is used to solve the problem. Not to mention that when we are in a reactive mindset we become more stressed and, as we saw earlier, will be less able to manage the crisis in a solution-focused manner.

We all have goals. Be it in the form of a bucket list, or more short-term goals such as climbing up the ladder at work, starting a family, or saving for a vacation. By setting goals and applying time management tools, you can be more successful in achieving these endeavors. Setting and attaining goals will be addressed in more detail later in this report.

Relationships become stronger by putting more time into them. By better managing your time, you can cultivate relationships that are healthy, happy, and mutually satisfying. Without as much stress in your life, you will bring a more positive attitude and be able to focus more on present interactions with others.

College students who have good time management skills are much more successful and achieve higher grades than those whose efficiency is poor. Students who can manage course work, exams, work, and socializing are the most productive and efficient. Not only are these students able to achieve great grades, they are also able to have much better social lives.

Good time management skills also improve your reputation. Those with poor skills in this area are frequently viewed as unreliable. Others may form the opinion that you are a liar who doesn't follow through with what you say you are going to do. Frequently, promises to others are broken as a result of not working efficiently and productively.

Lastly- when you are well organized and focused, tasks get done more quickly so you have more time to participate in activities of your choice. You may actually have leisure time. Break out the leisure suit! So by taking control of how our time is spent we can gain confidence, fun, peace of mind, sense of achievement, energy, better health, more family time and much, much, more.

Chapter 3: Getting started

"It's how we spend our time here and now, that really matters. If you are fed up with the way you have come to interact with time, change it." –
Marcia Wieder

SWOT analysis

A great way to get started in improving your time management skills is to complete a SWOT analysis. SWOT stands for strengths, weaknesses, opportunities, and threats.

By identifying these, you will be able to more accurately identify tools and strategies that will most benefit you. While completing this analysis, you will be reflecting on your skills in the areas of efficiency and productivity. Start by creating a list of your strengths and the impact each has, or could have, on your time management ability. When creating your list consider the following questions:

- What skills do I have?

- What education do I have?

- What can I do better than most other people?

- What would my boss, child, or spouse list as my strengths?

- What achievements am I most proud of?

- What values do I have that most other people do not?

Create another list of your weaknesses and how each of those might affect your skills in this area. While completing this it may be helpful to think about the answers to the following questions:

- What do I avoid doing?

- Why do I avoid doing certain tasks?

- Am I confident in my skills?

- What are some habits I have that limit my efficiency and productivity?

- What are the personality traits I have that impede my development of effective time management strategies?

When itemizing strengths and weaknesses you were listing those qualities within you that have a direct impact on time management. When creating lists of opportunities and threats, you will be reflecting on those things outside of yourself that have, or could have an impact, on reaching your time management goals. So create a list of opportunities that you could embrace and how each could assist you with improving your skills. Think about the following when you are working on this step:

- What technology do I have access to?

- Are there opportunities for growth in my current job?

- Is there a network of people who can help me or offer advice?

- Do I have educational opportunities that I can take advantage of?

The last step is to create a list of people or events that could hinder, or threaten, the effectiveness of any techniques or strategies you choose to use. Consider the answers to these questions when you are creating your list:

- What obstacles do I currently face at home?

- What obstacles do I currently face at work?

- Are there changes in my home or work lives that impact my effectiveness?

- Is technology threatening how I complete my job?

- Could any of my weaknesses result in threats?

Here is an example SWOT analysis to give you a basic idea of what to do (your lists should be much lengthier):

- Strengths

  - ❖ I am motivated to improve my skills in this area.
  - ❖ I have identified clear long- and short-term goals.
  - ❖ I have an ability to think logically in order to create an effective plan to achieve my goals

- Weaknesses

  - ❖ I have a tendency to procrastinate once I have identified the tasks I need to complete.
  - ❖ Throughout the day, I find myself distracted by surfing the internet and playing on-line games
  - ❖ I find myself spending extra time chatting on phone calls which takes time away from my projects

- Opportunities

  - ❖ My job provides several technological tools that I can use to increase my efficiency at work.
  - ❖ I have a great support system to help me with childcare if I need to get creative with scheduling.
  - ❖ The adult education program in my town routinely runs programs on time management.

- Threats

  - ❖ My children participate in many sports and want me to be present at their games frequently.
  - ❖ My cubicle is in a large room that has a tendency to be noisy and there is a lot of foot-traffic going past my desk throughout the day.
  - ❖ My boss does not have a tendency to clearly define projects he wants me to complete.

Determining how your time is used

When considering how your time is managed you must also determine how your time is spent on a daily and weekly basis.

If you are in a career this may involve projects, meetings, and appointments with clients. If you are a student, consider time spent in class, study time, work, commuting, and social aspects of life.   Knowing what you are doing is the key to determining how to lay out what you should be doing in order to complete tasks and accomplish your goals most efficiently.   So spend the couple of days prior to using new time management tools keeping a log of each and every activity, no matter how small, you complete during the day.   Along with that take note of:

- If it was scheduled in advance or not
- If the activity was interrupted
- Urgency
- Importance
- People involved with the task

With that information, you can determine many things including:

- How much time is spent in different areas of your life (work, family, social, recreational, spiritual, health, self-improvement)
- How many of the tasks completed were urgent
- How many of the tasks completed were important
- The people you spend the most time with
- How many of your activities are scheduled in advance
- How often you are interrupted and by who or what
- If there are activities you can cut back on
- If there are activities you can delegate or simplify
- If there are tasks that can be combined or grouped in such a way that will improve efficiency.

Using time, resources, knowledge, and technology

Time management is basically the process of manipulating tasks and time in order to be more efficient and productive. In order to become more effective at time management, you need to learn how to use time, resources, knowledge, and technology to your advantage.

As you previously read, determining how your time is being currently spent is a great starting point. Time can be manipulated further by getting organized, setting goals, and prioritizing. You can also work on managing your own time as well as managing other's time. To use other's time to your advantage you can delegate, train, educate, and outsource tasks as needed. We will talk more about this in a later chapter.

Knowing what resources are at your disposal and using them strategically is a great way to increase productivity. Recognize your own skills, talents, experiences, and ideas as valuable and use them. The SWOT analysis you may have completed earlier will assist you with this. Think about how can you improve them or use them to their highest potential?

Increasing your knowledge and level of education is much more efficient than using trial-and-error methods. Learning from mistakes is costly and can put your time budget in the negative. Mistakes are not highly efficient. There are four ways to use knowledge to your advantage:

1. Know what you need to learn
2. Know how much you need to learn
3. Be focused and selective
4. Take the time to learn

Using technology is another way to increase productivity. Adapt the technology you have to suit your needs. For example, if you are not a particularly talented typist, obtain voice recognition software and dictate reports, e-mails, etc.

If you spend time typing notes from meetings into your computer back at your office, use a laptop, PDA, or Smartphone application to take notes electronically during the meeting to avoid this step. Spreadsheets and data bases are frequently a very convenient way to access and manipulate large amounts of data concisely.

Chapter 4: Decision making

Time management sounds fairly easy and harmless. That is simply not true. Managing time effectively is extremely challenging in today's society when family, social, and work tasks have become so numerous. Other obstacles include poor decision making, over-scheduling, over-accessibility, and inability to determine the urgency of a task, distractibility, disorganization, not saying 'no', procrastination, fear of failure, perfectionism, depression, stress, and undefined goals. This chapter will help you to identify obstacles that may be hindering your ability to use valuable time much more effectively. Before addressing any decision-making task, ensure you are starting the process when you are in a calm and comfortable state of being. If you are stressed, decision making can become even more challenging. Clearly identify the specific result you are looking to get from your decision.

Some people have difficulty with time management due to challenges with decision making. Whether a decision is large or small, some people can get stuck and not be able to move on in order to accomplish a goal. Decision making can be even more challenging when a lot of information is unknown, there are many factors involved, the consequences are steep, there are many alternatives, or if it is a highly emotional topic.

Taking an organized approach to decision making allows all factors to be considered in an objective way. Here is an outline of a systematic approach to decision making:

- Create a calm, relaxed environment
- Clearly define your goal or objective
- Create a list of possible options to decide upon
- Process and think about each alternative
- Choose the best option
- Take action

There are several methods that can be used to generate ideas and alternative options for reaching a goal. Brainstorming is probably the most well-known option. This involves creating a list of all ideas to be considered. Reverse brainstorming is accomplished by coming up with ideas to achieve the opposite of what the true goal is. The actions are then reversed. If there are a lot of people involved in the decision making process the Charette Procedure can be used. In this procedure, a large number of people are divided into small groups. Each group brainstorms ideas in a sequential fashion until everyone involved has had a chance to contribute. Another way to generate ideas from a large amount of people is the Crawford Slip Writing Technique. Each person involved writes their idea, or ideas, on a slip of paper. The papers are collected and organized. This technique is beneficial for people who are not comfortable speaking aloud in a brainstorming session and also gives an estimate of the popularity of an idea if multiple people generate similar responses.

When ideas have been generated, it is helpful to organize them prior to analyzing the pros and cons of each. This can be done using several tools including an Affinity Diagram. Using this method, random ideas are categorized by theme. This can allow the decision-maker to identify common themes and connections between seemingly random ideas and also investigate the root causes and solutions to a problem.

After the organizational step, it is time to explore the alternatives. There are many, many ways to approach this process. The approach you choose will likely depend on what type of decision you are making and the amount of people involved in the process. If you have to choose between many alternatives, approach them two at a time in a paired comparison. Compare 1 and 2, if 2 is better, compare 2 to 3, if 2 is still better compare 2 to 4.

Use this elimination process until you are left deciding between 2 options. It is also sometimes helpful to create the traditional list of pro's and con's. This can help break a big decision into smaller, more manageable steps. If you are still struggling, remember that when you choose not to make a decision, you are making a decision. You've made a decision not to act.

Another way to explore the viability of an alternative is to conduct a risk analysis. A risk analysis model may be used when:

- Planning projects
- Deciding if a project should move forward
- Improving safety
- Preparing for harmful events
- Planning for changes

A risk analysis allows alternatives to be viewed in an objective fashion. Through this analysis, potential problems with a solution can be identified. These problems or threats can be related to human safety, operational functions, reputation, procedures, finances, technology, environmental, political, structural, or related to the problem itself. Then the probability of the threat occurring is estimated.

The following formula gives the value for risk:

Probability of event X Cost of threat occurring = Risk value.

Once the risk value is calculated, ways to manage the risk should be considered. Risks can often be managed using existing assets, creating a contingency plan, or obtaining new resources. Once this analysis has been completed for each possible alternative for the decision you making, the choice can be made based on the lowest risk value.

If a risk analysis is not quite what you are looking for, there are a couple other methods to look at the implications for each choice.

One such method is called Six Thinking Hats and was created by Edward de Bono. This technique is beneficial when looking at the effects of a decision from many different points of view. It allows emotion to be combined with objective analysis. The six hats are as follows:

- White Hat: This thinking hat focuses on analyzing the data and information that is available.

- Red Hat: This thinking hat focuses on looking at a problem in an intuitive or emotional way.

- Black Hat: This thinking hat focuses on looking at the negatives of the decision. Identifying why a solution may not work.

- Yellow Hat: This thinking hat focuses on looking at the positives of the decision.

- Green Hat: This thinking hat focuses on identifying creative solutions to a problem.

- Blue Hat: This thinking hat focuses on controlling the process of idea gathering and decision making.

The decision making skills you have learned in this chapter will be invaluable during the processes of goal setting and prioritizing that you will do later on.

Chapter 5: Goal Setting

"If you want to live a happy life, tie it to a goal, not to people or things." ~ *Albert Einstein*

Setting goals is imperative in time management. Not only do they allow us to increase our efficiency and productivity, they make us feel better. People who work hard and achieve their goals feel confident, in control, and motivated. These are key traits of those who attain a high level of success in their lives. Setting goals can be rather complex. By reading this chapter, you should gain the skills needed to set positive, meaningful, and achievable goals.

The most important thing to do when establishing goals in your life is to make sure that they are important to YOU. Many times, goals get set because they are important to others. Maybe a goal is set to earn a promotion at work. This goal should be set because you want the promotion, not because your spouse does or your boss has recommended you to pursue advancing your career. There are also certain cultural expectations around physical health, family, and socializing. People may set goals in order to meet society's expectations, not their own expectations. In order to get motivated and achieve a goal it must be important and relevant to you. It must also be in-line with your personal values and ethics.

It is also imperative that new goals you create do not contradict or impede the achievement of goals you have already set. For example, if you have set a goal to lose 5% of your body weight by May 2013, also setting a goal to try every restaurant within a 25-mile radius of your home by May 2013 would be detrimental to the achievement of your first goal. This type of goal sabotage is often referred to as non-integrated thinking and should be avoided.

"Balance is not better time management, but better boundary management. Balance means making choices and enjoying those choices." – *Betsy Jacobson*

Make sure you create goals that focus on different facets of your life. All too often, a person will create goals only focusing solely on health or only on work. In order to achieve balance in life and integrate the various aspects of it, it is important to consider many different areas including:

- Family and home
- Spiritual and ethical
- Physical and health
- Social and cultural
- Mental and educational

As you are preparing to make positive changes in your life, it is important that the goals you set to make these changes are also framed positively. We want to send our conscious and subconscious minds strong, positive messages in order to achieve success. For example, instead of writing the goal "I will stop procrastinating and accomplish 5 tasks on my to-do list each day", re-work it in a more positive framework to say, "I will use my new skills in order to accomplish 5 tasks on my to-do list each day". Think positively for a positive outcome.

Start your goal setting projects by dreaming big. What are some things you want to do or accomplish over the long-term? These could be related to a career, money, education, family, creativity, spirituality, socializing, personal growth, achievements, physicality, public service, or simply for fun. It is important that goals are set high enough so we feel good after working so hard to achieve them. That said- make sure they are not so high that you feel overwhelmed and start thinking that you are failing.

In 1968, Dr. Edwin Locke published an article called "Toward a Theory of Task Motivation and Incentives". This article describes the results of his research in the area of goal setting and motivation. He determined that people, employees in his study, were highly motivated by clear goals and by receiving feedback during the goal achievement process. He concluded that a person's productivity or performance was significantly improved by setting goals. Further study in this area determined that specific, challenging goals most often resulted in success compared to goals that were simple and/or vague.

In 1990, Locke combined forces with Dr. Gary Latham to publish a book, "A Theory of Goal Setting and Task Performance" which outlined the characteristics of good goal setting. They determined that in order for a goal to be motivating, it must have 5 characteristics. The first quality is clarity. By this, Locke and Latham mean that goals should be very clear, concise, and specific. It should be easily understood. Having a clear goal also means that we are able to measure our progress and know, with absolute certainty, when it has been achieved. They also stated that goals must be challenging. This means that we need to set goals that require a significant amount of work so we have a sense of accomplishment upon its achievement. It also refers to the fact that the goal must be personally relevant and rewarding. Commitment is another aspect of goal setting that they addressed. Everyone who is involved with the goal and its achievement must agree with and understand the goal. Locke and Latham also reported that receiving feedback while working toward a goal was very important. This feedback serves to clarify expectations and methods to ensure productivity and efficiency. Also, people who receive recognition for their achievements tend to be more motivated and successful. Task complexity is also a feature that they addressed. Although tasks should be challenging, they should not be overwhelming. That may mean allocating more resources or allowing more time for its achievement.

A goal writing tool that can go along with Locke and Latham's theory is the SMART method of goal setting as described on mindtools.com. The method is actually a mnemonic device outlined here:

- S- Specific
- M- Measurable
- A- Attainable

- R- Relevant or rewarding
- T- Trackable

By creating goals that have all of these qualities, you are insuring that they are clear and motivating. For example, some might set the goal of traveling to Europe. That goal lacks specificity, work towards it is not able to be tracked, and it is not measurable. Using the SMART method your goal of "travel to Europe" would change into "Save $2,000 to travel to Europe in May 2016".

Now that you have some great ideas for creating goals here are some things to avoid when goal setting:

- Making goals unrealistic
- Focusing on too few areas- include many facets of your life
- Underestimating completion time
- not appreciating failure
- setting goals because others are imposing them on you
- Not tracking progress or looking back to see what progress has been made
- Setting negative goals
- Setting too many goals

Once long-term goals are set you can break each of these down into more manageable steps. Put these steps on order of priority (we will talk about how to do this a little later). Decide if you want the steps broken down into daily, weekly, or monthly to-do lists (more on this later too). These will depend on the long-term goals you have.

Once you have set some goals, read on to learn about ways to prioritize and manage your time while working to achieve them.

Chapter 6: Prioritizing

Prioritizing is a key skill in time management. One way to complete your to do list is using a first in, first out approach. Tasks go on the list and get completed in order without regard for importance or urgency. Let us re-visit the Pareto principle again. Say you have a to-do list with 10 items on it. According to the Pareto principle, only 2 of these are likely to be important. So what would happen if these items happened to be last on our to-do list for the day and we ran out of time while completing the first 8? The answer is, we would not have accomplished what is most important and efficient therefore undermining the whole process of improving time management to become more productive. Consider thinking of success not by the number of the tasks you accomplish, but the importance of the tasks you accomplish. If you can prioritize effectively, you will minimize stress, maximize efficiency, and achieve your goals.

When deciding whether or not a task is of a high priority, or worth completing it at all, reflect on the following questions:

- What would happen if I didn't do this?
- Will doing this have a benefit in the future?
- Why am I doing it?
- Does it matter if I do it?
- Is this in-line with my personal beliefs and values?

The Action Priority Matrix

One way to prioritize is to use the Action Priority Matrix. Firstly, determine the importance of the activity. Importance is how vital the activity is to achieving your goals. Urgency is another factor to consider. This relates to the time constraints of a task but may not necessarily reflect the achievement of a goal. Some activities can be urgent and important, important but non urgent, urgent but not important, and some are not urgent and also not important. Thinking in this way can help to prioritize tasks. Activities that are deemed urgent and important can stem from two things; lack of planning or crisis. If you find that many of your important and urgent tasks are the result of poor planning, this is where your focus should be in your overall improvement of time management skills. If an activity is urgent and not important, decide if the task can be rescheduled or delegated to someone else. Most of our tasks should be classified as important and not urgent for maximum effectiveness. Activities that are classified as not important and not urgent can be labeled as distractions and dealt with as such.

ABCD methods

The ABCD method of prioritization can also be used (www.timethoughts.com). You will need your to-do list, master task, or master project list to use this technique. Each entry on the list is assigned a letter as follows:

- A- Tasks that are important and urgent (have a deadline) are assigned an A.

- B- Tasks that need to be accomplished but are not urgent are assigned a B.

- C- Tasks that are under consideration for future completion are assigned a C.

- D- Tasks that have come across your desk but you are not planning to do are assigned a D.

Once each task has a letter, assign priority rankings to the A's (A1, A2, etc). If you believe two tasks have equal weight, assign them the same number. Start with A's with the highest priority and work your way up the alphabet and number line as your day, week, or month progresses.

Let us talk about one other alphabetical approach to prioritization. This one was designed by Brian Tracy. Each task is given a priority level as follows:

- Priority A- Things you must be doing
- Priority B- Things you should be doing
- Priority C- Things it would be nice to do
- Priority D- Things to delegate
- Priority E- Things to eliminate

Now that you have prioritized goals, keep on going to learn how to schedule the tasks associated with their achievement.

Chapter 7: Scheduling

Scheduling should start by deciding how much time is going to be allotted for different types of tasks or different areas of our lives. Theorists have come up with several approaches to this.

Deciding what to schedule

Decide what you are going to schedule. Are you going to simply put down set appointments that you must attend and keep a to-do list for daily tasks separately? Are you planning on scheduling each task you need to complete each day? There are a couple different schools of thought on how much time should be devoted to different types of activities in a daily schedule. One way to do it is as follows:

- For this method, 8 hours for sleep are removed from the equation when taking into account the amount of time available to a person.
- All tasks are divided into categories:

- Necessities- The tasks you need to accomplish in order to keep your home and work environments functioning.

- Give- The tasks you accomplish to give something or do something for someone else.

- Long term success- The tasks you need to accomplish in order to meet the long-term goals you have set.

- Education- The tasks you need to accomplish to meet your self-improvement and educational goals.

- Financial Freedom- The time you spend increasing your wealth and making money (in addition to your "day job")

- Play- The time you set aside for leisure, rest, and relaxation.

Assign each category a percentage of time for each week:

- Necessities- 55% of your time or 61 hours a week

- Give- 5% of your time or 5 hours a week

- Long term success- 10% of your time or 11 hours a week

- Education- 10% of your time or 11 hours a week

- Financial freedom- 10% of your time or 11 hours a week

- Play- 10% of your time or 11 hours a week

Pickle jar theory

"I attended a seminar once where the instructor was lecturing on time. At one point, he said, "Okay, it's time for a quiz." He reached under the table and pulled out a wide-mouth gallon jar. He set it on the table next to a platter with some fist-sized rocks on it. "How many of these rocks do you think we can get in the jar?" he asked.

After we make our guess, he said, "Okay, let's find out." He set one rock in the jar...then another...then another. I don't remember how many he got in, but he got the jar full. Then he asked, "Is the jar full?" Everybody looked at the rocks and said, "Yes."

Then he said, "Ahh." He reached under the table and pulled out a bucket of gravel. Then he dumped some gravel in and shook the jar, and the gravel went in all the little spaces left by the big rocks. Then he grinned and said once more, "Is the jar full?" By this time we were on to him. "Probably not," we said."Good!" he replied. And he reached under the table and brought out a bucket of sand. He started dumping the sand in and it went in all the little spaces left by the rocks and gravel. Once more he looked at us and said, "Is the jar full?" "No!" we all roared. He said, "Good!" and he grabbed a pitcher of water and began to pour it in. He got something like a quart of water in that jar. Then he said, "Well, what's the point?" Somebody said, "Well, there are gaps and if you really work at it, you can always fit more into your life." "No," he said, "that's not the point. The point is this: if you hadn't put these big rocks in first, you would never have gotten any of them in!"

Covey, S.R., Merrill, A.R., and Merrill, R.R. First things first. New York: Simon & Shuster; 1994, pp. 88-89.

The pickle jar theory is a visualization strategy for time management. To start using this technique, think about taking a pickle jar and filling it with rather large rocks. These rocks represent major goals and responsibilities in life. If we reflect back to Maslow, these are the steps at the bottom of the pyramid. For some people the large rocks might include parenting or career responsibilities. These large rocks should be scheduled first and high on a priority list. Next, imagine that the spaces between the rocks are filled in with pebbles. This makes the jar appear fuller. The pebbles represent our hobbies and leisure activities, they don't take up as much room as the rocks, but they are still a prominent feature in the jar. Pebbles could be reading, watching television, or playing guitar. There are still spaces that could be filled by sand, try to visualize that. These grains of sand represent our daily chores and activities such as washing dishes, showering, and pumping gas. After the sand has been added, the remaining spaces that are barely visible could be filled by water. The water symbolizes the things that distract us or could be considered the 'time wasters' in our life. We will talk much more about these a little later.

Pareto's Principle

Pareto's Principle offers us a very different perspective. It was suggested by Joseph Juran, a business management consultant and was modeled after work completed by Italian economist Vilfredo Pareto. This principle is also known as the 80-20 Rule, the Law of the Vital Few, and the Principle of Factor Sparsity. In 1906, Vilfredo Pareto, created a mathematic formula demonstrating the unequal distribution of wealth in Italy. He calculated that 80% of the land in Italy was owned by 20% of the people in Italy.

This is now a common general rule in business, that is, 80% of your sales come from 20% of your customers. To apply this principle to life management, it has been suggested that only 20% of the things we own or what we do in life actually matter. Therefore, focusing on that 20% will allow us to be more efficient and happy. So let's think about how this rule might affect a person's morning routine. Consider the following 10 tasks:

- Tooth brushing
- Eating breakfast
- Tying shoes
- Make a phone call to request needed information
- Washing dishes
- Making coffee
- Taking a shower
- Walking the dog
- Locking the door
- Starting a load of laundry

If we apply the 80/20 rule to this scenario, many people would be most productive and happy if they focused on the phone call and dog walking. The other tasks are rather mundane with little productive or 'feel good' payout. On the other hand- making the phone call will allow the rest of the day to run more efficiently and many people enjoy a morning walk with their dog to clear their heads and boost their energy levels.

50-30-20 rule

The 50-30-20 rule is another mathematical representation that is outlined by Steve Pavlina on his website. Pavlina suggests that tasks can be classified into three types. Further, he proposes the percentage of time that should be spent on tasks within each category. It is described as follows:

- A Tasks- This category refers to goals or achievements that can be accomplished in 5 years or more. Pavlina suggests that we spend 50% of our time on these tasks. Examples of A Tasks include:

  ❖ Buying a home
  ❖ Achieving a management level job
  ❖ Earning an advanced college degree

- B Tasks- This category refers to goals or achievements that can be accomplished within 2 years. Pavlina suggests we spend 30% of our time on these tasks. Examples of B Tasks include:

  ❖ Learning a foreign language
  ❖ Saving for a luxury vacation
  ❖ Having a child

- C Tasks- This category refers to goals or achievements that can be accomplished in 90 days or less. Pavlina suggests that we spend 20% of our time on these tasks. Examples of C Tasks include:

- ❖ Take an enrichment course
- ❖ Establish an exercise plan
- ❖ Improve productivity at work by 30%

Time Estimating

The next step of scheduling is to determine how much time you need in order to complete a particular task. Before determining the amount of time that is needed you must:

- Know what is required

- Prioritize activities and tasks

- Decide who needs to be involved in task completion

There are several different methods that can be used to determine how much time is needed for the accomplishment of a certain task.

One technique is taking your current to-do list and jotting down the time you think it will take to accomplish each task. Once that is done, complete the tasks and note how long it actually takes you to complete them. Then, add up the time you spent on the task, divide it by your estimated time and you have your "fudge ratio" (www.stevepavlina.com). So whenever you calculate the amount of time needed to complete a task, make your best guess and add your fudge ratio to it to increase your accuracy.

Bottom-up estimating can also be effective. This allows you to determine the amount of time a whole project will take by breaking it down to smaller tasks and estimating time for each step. The opposite approach, top-down estimating requires developing a vague outline for task accomplishment and using past experience to guide your judgment for how long the entire project will take.

If those methods do not appeal to you here are a few more. To use a comparative estimating procedure look at the time it took you to complete similar tasks in the past and base your estimations on that. When using parametric estimating, guess at the time it will take to complete one piece of the task and multiply that by the number of tasks to be completed to achieve the ultimate goal. Three-point estimation can also be used. This involves making three estimates. The first is your best case scenario, the second is the worst case, and the third is the most reasonable or likely.

Creating a schedule

Some people create a schedule at the beginning of every week. Others create one at the end of each day for the next day. Still others create one for the current day every morning. The best advice is to do what works for you and once you figure out what works- stick with it.

If you are looking for a highly structured, traditional schedule you may want to try this approach and follow these steps:

1. Determine how much time you have available
2. Add in the activities that are of highest priority or absolutely have to occur at a set time.
3. Look at your to-do list and schedule in high priority activities that are urgent
4. Establish blocks of time in which to deal with the unforeseen or miscalculations of the amount of time it will take to complete a task.
5. Fill-in the remaining activities in your to-do list based on priority.

Now, it is not necessary to schedule every minute of every day. For some people, setting a weekly to-do list is enough to keep them on track. Others need daily or monthly task lists. People with many appointments, meetings, or classes are likely to benefit the most from a more fine-tuned daily agenda.

Scheduling blocks of time is another strategy that works for some people. You might block 2 hours for "you time", 1 hour for "education time", and 2 hours for "chores" for example. This gives some flexibility in how that time is spent but insures balance with regard to how much time you are spending on different types of tasks.

The Pomodoro Technique was developed by Francesco Cirillo in the 1980s. This technique incorporates time period of focused work with frequent breaks to keep the mind sharp throughout the day. This technique works as follows:

A. Identify a task to accomplish
B. Set the pomodoro (timer) for 25 minutes
C. Work on the task until the timer goes off.
D. Mark an X on a piece of paper
E. Take a 5 minute break
F. Begin back at b.
G. When you have four X's on your paper, take a 15-20 minute break

No matter how you decide to schedule your time, consider the following tips and tricks to improve efficiency and productivity:

- Work in blocks of time- around 50 minutes with set break-times

- Create dedicated study or work spaces

- Conduct weekly progress reviews

- Postpone unimportant or non-urgent tasks until after the work is completed

- Identify resources for help- tutors, friends, websites, professionals, professional organizations. This save time, energy, and allows for fresh input into problem solving

- Review notes and readings just before a class or meeting

- Review notes just after a class or meeting

Reminders

Some people may find that they need reminders throughout the day to stick to a schedule. There are several strategies that can be used to trigger your memory in order to meet your goals in a timely manner. Firstly, you can do something out of the ordinary that will trigger a thought. This is the old "tying a string around your finger" trick. This could also be a sticker on your desk or a band aid on your arm. The trick is to associate it with a task so when you view the item, you are sparked into thinking about the task. Repetition is the key. Repeating the details of an appointment to yourself over and over again can help it to stick. It might also be helpful to write it down a number of times. For those creative types, writing a rhyme or a song to remember information can be beneficial. You could also invest heavily in sticky notes. Put reminders or information and stick them wherever you need them including on your computer, in your purse, on your steering wheel, on your front door, or on the bathroom mirror - whatever makes sense to you. Creating a visual association is helpful for some people. Think of a detailed picture involving all of your senses in order to trigger a memory. For example, if you are meeting a friend for dinner at a restaurant at 7 o'clock, picture sitting at the restaurant and smelling the lovely food. The waiter comes over and spills a drink on your friend. The stain left on your friend's shirt looks like a 7. If you are in need of strategies specifically for being on time, consider setting your clock ahead or setting multiple alarms. Time timers are visual countdown timers with a red section representing the amount of time you have left. When the red is gone, your time is up.

Now that you have decided how to schedule, read on to take a look at tools to document your schedule and help you stick to it.

Chapter 8: Planners and personal organizers

There are many different time management systems available through the internet and at stores. This chapter will share several of those options for you.   Many people have tried, and failed, to improve their time management skills by applying the use of several tools or strategies.   There are several reasons why these attempts might fail.   Firstly, the system could be too complex.   It would certainly be overwhelming for a person who is used to keeping to-do lists and calendars in a paper format and making the change to doing all of these things electronically. Not only may this be too complex, it might not be the user's style. Above all else, the tools you choose must suit you.   Having multiple schedules for example, one for work, one for family, one for personal appointments and activities, can be too complex and ineffective.   This would not only be complex, but also redundant.   Redundancy is another reason that a time management technique might not work.   A good system would have one, and only one, of the following:

- address book
- calendar
- to-do list
- notebook

A lack of accessibility can also impede the effectiveness of a technique.   Is a planner too big?   Trouble remembering to leave the house with your schedule, to-do list, notebook etc.?   If so, these tools would not be effective and could be deemed ineffective.

The biggest decision to make when deciding on a planner is to choose a paper-based or electronic-based system.   Both have their advantages.   Electronic planners allow you to:

- Edit easily and quickly
- Search quickly
- portable
- audible or visual alerts
- Computer backup
- Keeps lists organized and accessible

- Most screens are lit and can be used in the dark
- May integrate with a device you already own (cell phone, smart phone, itouch, etc.)

Paper planners provide:

- The ability to view everything at one time
- Change your writing or circle items to make important things stand out
- If you are the type of person that can remember where on a page you wrote something, you can easily flip through and find what it is you are looking for.
- You do not need to learn any new skills
- The batteries will not die
- Technology will not become obsolete

Paper planners come in a couple different general styles. Some come in a binder with pre-printed pages. This format has a couple of advantages. Firstly, you can re-arrange the pages and sections according to your preferences. Re-fill pages in a variety of formats can also be purchased, or sometimes even printed offline, meaning it will never fill-up to the point where you have to trash or file it and start over. The disadvantage to using a binder is size and structure. A large workspace is needed to use one because it cannot fold back on itself, like say a spiral bound notebook would. They also tend to be heavier due to the metal in the mechanics.

A hardbound notebook is also an option. If you choose to use one, look for one with pockets in the front and/or back to put notes, receipts, telephone messages, etc. into. These notebooks tend to be sturdy and lightweight. They require the same amount of space as a binder and have the disadvantage of not being able to lay out flat on a surface. Pages cannot be re-arranged or refilled meaning that before purchasing you must pay special attention to the order of the pages, categories, information etc. Also, if you find on you like buy a couple so that once you fill the first one you will have others in case it becomes hard to find or discontinued.

Another option is a spiral-bound notebook. These are extremely affordable and flexible to bend and use. That said, they tend to fall apart more easily than other formats and, like the hardbound notebooks, do not have the advantage of being re-arranged or refilled.

The last option is a disc bound planner. In these, pages are bound using a series of loose, thin hubs. Paper is punched into a mushroom-shape and the discs are fastened in the cross-section. Their innovative design allows them to fold over onto themselves, making them convenient and usable in a variety of environments. They are usually made of plastic, eliminating the weight associated with metal bindings. Pages can be re-arranged and re-filled as per your preferences. In this format, discs are always evenly spaced allowing you to use several different-sized pages within the same binder.

The disadvantage of this type is they are not quite as sturdy and durable as a hardbound notebook.

Many calendars and personal organizers have options to present information in a daily, weekly, or monthly format. Monthly systems work best for getting a general overview of the coming weeks. Keeping track of bill due dates, travel, holidays, and deadlines are well presented in this format. Frequently, if you prefer this method you will also want to incorporate a daily or weekly organizer in order to track more detailed information. Weekly planners are probably the most popular as they allow for both daily planning and an overview of the entire week. Depending on the particular one, information may be presented in columns (vertical or horizontal) and some will include notation sections. Daily planners, sometimes called page-a-day planners, focus specifically on the current day. They can track appointments, phone calls, expenses, to-do lists, and a lot of other information. The down side is not being able to look ahead and visualize larger units of time easily. All in all if you are looking for long-range planning abilities, use a monthly format. If you want to record a lot of detail on a daily basis, use a daily planner. If you are in between, use a weekly planner.

Remember- a combination is OK but don't let your system get too complex.

Some people may choose to use an electronic organizer. Electronic organizers can be referred to as PDAs, Personal Digital Assistant. These are frequently being replaced however by Smartphones and tablets equipped with time management applications. There are several formats to use in order to have an electronic calendar. These include software on your computer such as Microsoft Calendar, as well as on-line formats such as Google calendar. These can be integrated with e-mail in order to receive reminders which can be helpful to many people. Before deciding on an electronic organizer it is important to consider what you will use it for. Options for use include:

- Supplementing a paper organizer
- All-in-one phone, organizer, mp3 player
- Extensive note taking
- Web access
- Access to e-mail
- Keeping appointments
- To-do lists
- Store phone numbers
- Calendar
- Memo pad

Once you decide what you want to use it for, decide what features you are looking for. Common features to consider include:

- Screen size
- Battery life
- Size
- Weight
- Processor speed
- Web capability
- Phone capability
- Memory
- Keyboard type

- Keyboard size
- Touch screen
- Operating system compatibility

When several key features have been identified, use a website specializing in technology to search for devices with these features. Then, check out product review websites prior to making your purchase.

Once you have made your decision and purchased the planning tool of your choice, read on to learn how to fill it with the vital information you will need to further increase your time management ability.

Chapter 9: Lists, lists, and more lists
To-do lists

To-do lists are simply a simple way to present tasks that need to be accomplished. It is fluid and flexible, shortening and lengthening as you complete tasks and add more. They are an invaluable tool for many people. To-do lists keep us on track by organizing the tasks we need to complete on a daily or weekly basis. Being able to cross items out as they are completed is highly rewarding intrinsically and can result in an amazing feeling of satisfaction and achievement. To-do lists also provide back-up for frequently failing and unstable memory capabilities.

To-do lists should be portable and easily accessible. These lists can help reduce stress, remind us of what needs to be done, helps us focus, and allows us to strategize a plan of attack on a daily (or weekly) basis. Spending 15 minutes at the end of each day to create a to-do list for the next day is an invaluable use of your time.

To-do lists can be tricky. It takes some work to determine what is most beneficial for you to include on them and what your time-frame for the list will be. Here are a couple options for to-do lists structures:

- Include tasks that can be completed in one sitting
- Include tasks that need more than one sitting to complete
- Include tasks that need to be started on a particular day
- Include tasks that need to be finished on a particular day
- Include tasks that are important
- Include tasks that are not important
- Include appointments

Some people keep one list, some people keep several. Some people have a list for each and every day while some people have a list for a week. Instead of making a to-do list and tackling it from top to bottom, try to prioritize it first. Take your large, master to-do list and transfer over the 5 most important things to be accomplished the next day. Rank each item from 1-5 in order of importance. Jot down how much time you estimate it will take you to complete each task. The next day, start with item #1, your most important task, and complete it. Then move onto item #2 and so on until you have completed all 5 tasks. Prioritization can also be done by highlighting or color-coding, just make sure to keep it simple.

Action lists

In addition to having a to-do list, some people like to create longer-term action lists. Writing an action plan outlines the steps towards achieving a goal. First, use the techniques described earlier to write a clear and motivational goal. Then, write down all the actions or steps you may need to take in order to achieve the goal. Doing this using a brainstorming technique, you are not looking to judge or analyze at this point. Now that you have your list of actions, it is time to choose those that are most effective and necessary. Drop any actions from your list that are not necessary. Organize the list into a plan by deciding on the order in which they should be completed. Begin following your plan and review and revise it as necessary.

Project lists

If you have several large(ish) projects going you may find that creating a master list is helpful in order to keep track of them. The master project list can be used as a starting point for creating plans for the completion of a project when it is time to start tackling it. In turn, items from the project plan can be used in a daily or weekly to-do list.

SuperFocus Notebook system

On his blog, time management Mark Forester introduces his SuperFocus Notebook system. Here are the steps to using it:

- Get a notebook
- On the left side of the page create a list of the tasks you need to do. Leave room for a second column on the right hand side of the page as you use this process, add additional tasks when you think of them or they are assigned.
- Starting at the top of the list, think about each task until you reach one that you feel ready to work on.
- Work on that task for as long as you can or feel like it
- Go back to your notebook. If you completed the tasks cross it out with a horizontal line. If it is not finished cross it out but write the task again in the right hand column of the next page.
- Urgent tasks are entered in the right hand column (column 2) of the page you are currently working on.
- Continue working on tasks on the first page until no more can be done.
- All tasks in column 2 must be completed before going onto the next page.

Mindmapping

If you are a highly creative and visual person, you may like to use a Mindmapping technique for creating a to-do list. This technique is presented in the book "Mindmapping" by Joyce Wycoff. Mind Maps are flexible, interactive, colorful, and reflect a thinking process. In order to create a Mind Map you need:

- Paper
- Pen
- Yellow highlighter
- Pink highlighter

Mind Maps work best when they are created at the beginning of the week and are updated on a daily basis. Start the process by drawing a circle, or a rectangle, in the middle of the page. In the shape, write "To Do" and add the date range for the week you are mapping. Next, draw a line out from the center and label it "goals". Then divide tasks that you need to accomplish into categories and draw a line out from the center for each category (preferably using a different color for each category). Out of these sub-branches (goals and categories) draw lines branching out with the tasks you want to accomplish relating to each area. Now you have created your Mind Map. At the beginning of each day, use the yellow highlighter and highlight the tasks you would like to accomplish that day. If you desire, you can number each one to give them a priority ranking. Once you have completed a task it is highlighted in pink. Here is a picture of a Mind Map from www.usingmindmaps.com

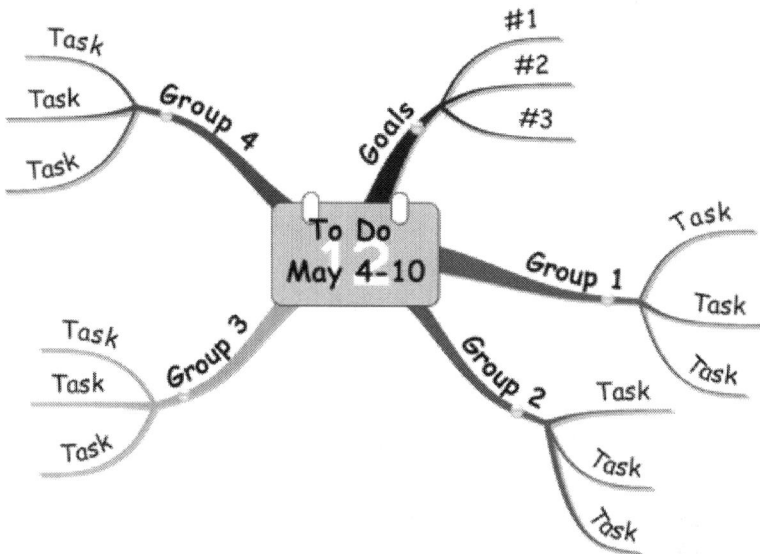

After trying Mind Mapping on paper, you can begin to explore software options as well.

Chapter 10: Organization

Disorganization at home or in the work space leads to wasted time for several reasons. First off, information or items you need are not easily accessible and thus time is wasted locating them. In fact, the National Association of Professional Organizers reports that the average person spends about one year of our lives looking for lost items. Also, when we work in a disorganized environment, it is often hard to remain focused and motivated to work. If those reasons aren't enough to spark you into action consider this- it costs about $10 per square foot to store items in your house.

Follow these tips to increase organization in your home or office:

- Make a list of areas that need to be organized
- Pick a starting point. Try to choose an area that will have the most impact on your efficiency when organized

- Set a deadline
- Recruit some help

In order to be truly organized, your space cannot just look tidy. If someone opens a closet or drawer, they too should be neat. And neat is only part of it- organization refers to a structured system that allows things to look neat and also allow you to locate items easily when needed. IT also involves not storing and wasting time with things that you do not need. Consider that the average America receives 49,060 pieces of mail in a lifetime. It would not be considered efficient or organized to save and file all that. Especially considering that about 1/3 of it is unsolicited junk mail.

Julie Morganstern, in her book "Organizing from the Inside Out", presents the SPACE method for organization. To use this model, you start by Sorting like or similar items into groups. You then Purge and get rid of unneeded items. The next step is to Assign every item a place. Assigning can be done while Containerizing, or creating an appropriate storage method. The last step is to Equalize by frequently re-evaluating if your system is working for you.

Once you have decided on a space to organize, be it a closet, office, bedroom, or locker, start by throwing away or donating all items that you don't often use. Ask yourself:

- Do I really need this?
- Have I used it in the past year?
- Will I use it in the coming year?
- Do I love it?
- Could someone else use the object more?
- Will I miss it if I don't have it?
- If I don't have it can I replace it easily?
- Could it be better placed in another room?

Make sure all remaining objects have a clearly defined, and handy, place to be kept. Make sure the most frequently used items are placed somewhere where you can get to them and replace them easily. If the placement of an object is not convenient for you, the system is likely to fail. Feel free to try different place until you find what works for you. It is particularly handy to have a consistent specific place for a purse/wallet, cell phone, and keys.

Once everything has a place, get into the routine of putting it back as soon as you are finished with it to reduce clutter and so that you will know exactly where it is the next time you need it.

Part of the organization of things is storage. In order to have things stored well, they must be sorted and filed. Before the storage process begins however, the purging process needs to occur. People in general have a tendency to save too much stuff. In order to begin sorting the keeps from the items to be placed in the circular file (a.k.a. trash can), items currently being used for projects can be placed in a project file. Start a project file for each active project you are work on. Then sort through the remainder. Use this general guide- anything you keep should not be part of a current project and is something that you estimate a high probability for using in the future. Ask yourself if the item is valuable enough to go through the process of filing, storing, managing, and organizing it.

When you have all your keepers decide where and how you are going to store your information. Files are best organized in either an alphabetical or category-based fashion. Consider on separating frequently used files from those that are very rarely used. Periodically go through your files to be sure they are still relevant and worth saving. A file of "tickler folders" can also be used. First, create a folder for each month of the year. You will then make 31 subfolders for each month, one for each day. File items that need to be accessible on a particular day in the corresponding folder. At the beginning of the day, remove the needed file. At the end of the day, file uncompleted work into the next day's file.

These days, electronic files are used frequently. The key to saving these files is storing them in such a way that they can be easily located. One way to do this is using a hierarchical directory structure. To do this, all documents and files related to a particular project, person, or event is organized into a single folder. Within that folder, subfolders can be created by topic. Topic folders can contain function folders. Function folders can contain activity folders relating to the activity in the function folder. Make sure that when saving documents and folders, a consistent naming pattern is used - using a date can frequently be helpful. As you would avoid filing unneeded paper documents, avoid saving unnecessary electronic documents. As we know that computers can fail, make sure your files are backed up.

On her website, www.time-management-coach.com, Claire Tompkins presents her time management system. One method she proposes is the inbox system. Get some sort of 'inbox' and put EVERYTHING in it. Mail, scraps of paper with notes jotted on them, meeting notes, phone messages, etc. The next step is the process the contents of the inbox. Decide if each item requires an action or can be filed. If you decide that an action is necessary and it can be accomplished in a single step (quick phone call or e-mail) complete it immediately. If it is more time consuming then add it to your to-do list. If it is part of a long-term project add it to the list of steps you have created to complete the project. If it is something someone else can manage, delegate the task.

Chapter 11: Interruptions and other distractions

Let us start this chapter on interruptions and distractions by discriminating between the two. An interruption is something beyond your control that requires you to stop what you are doing and react. A distraction is something we give our attention to willingly, at the cost of stopping whatever we were working on. For example, if someone walks into your office and starts a conversation with you, it would not be alright to ignore him or her. This is an interruption. If you are working at your computer and notice a new e-mail has come in and you stop what you are doing to check it, you have been distracted.

Being constantly interrupted can have a great impact on maintaining a schedule and working efficiently. If you find that you are frequently being interrupted start by keeping data on when and where you are interrupted as well as what or who the distracter is. Look for patterns. Is your boss popping into your office and interrupting you? Letting people know when you are 'available' or 'unavailable' can be very helpful. A sign on the door, posted "office hours", or simply an open door can give people information as to when they can reach you. If you are consistently interrupted by phone calls, try starting conversations with "I only have x number of minutes to talk"

"Distractions are costly: A temporary shift in attention from one task to another – stopping to answer an e-mail or take a phone call, for instance – increases the amount of time necessary to finish the primary task by as much as 25%, a phenomenon known as "switching time". It's far more efficient to fully focus for 90 to 120 minutes, take a true break, and then fully focus on the next activity." Tony Schwartz, Manage your energy, not your time – Harvard Business Review.

The first thing to consider when it comes to distractions is realizing that you can choose to react to or ignore the stimulus. Unlike with interruptions, you have complete control over your response.

Are you distracted by the phone ringing? Texts? E-mails? Determine patterns and address them. Using your voicemail to screen calls allows you to listen at an appropriate time, determine the call's importance and urgency and then respond appropriately. Turn off e-mail notifications so you can check them at a predetermined time or frequency. If you use a program such as Outlook, you set a rule so the program only checks the server for messages at certain times.

If you do not need the internet, it is highly recommended that you disconnect it. This way you will not get sucked in by the biggest time-waster that has ever existed. If you do need the internet, consider using a program that blocks out predetermined time wasting sites. Programs like Invisibility Cloak or Kiwi Cloak may be worth a try. A program like Time to Go only allows you to surf a website for a set amount of time.

If you work in a cubicle, share an office, or work on a busy hallway consider wearing headphones while you work. You can put them on with no noise coming through or you could try instrumental music or white noise. Wearing headphones may have the added benefit of inhibiting others from interrupting you.

Working in a clutter free environment is another way to stay focused and reduce distractions. This includes computer clutter as well as desk and other environmental debris. See the chapter on organization for more tips on this subject.

If you find yourself being distracted by your own thoughts consider meditating. This is a great way to help your brain quiet itself. To do this, take a few deep breaths while your eyes are closed and focus on breathing. Let your thoughts pass through your brain fluidly, not letting anyone stick around. If one thought does get stuck, bring your attention back to your breath. Do this until you feel more focused and centered.

Reflective writing is another way to re-focus. Writing improves mindfulness by slowing down time. By writing, thoughts become ordered and have increased clarity. The writing process also separates reason from emotion and allows for a different perspective to form. Reflective writing sessions last between 5 and 10 minutes. A pen and paper or a computer can be used. Do not worry about editing, just get the ideas out. The goal is to reflect on a decision, an error, a problem, or a process.

Here are some other ideas for reflective writing:

- Re-tell the situation from someone else's perspective
- Answer a "what if" question
- Go ahead and rant
- Script a conversation
- Give yourself feedback on a recently accomplished task
- Draw diagrams to visually represent a problem or concept
- Write a story about a recent experience
- Create an action plan

Improving concentration

Increasing your mental concentration capacity is a great way to improve productivity. And the best thing is- you will always have it with you unlike other tools that are external. When looking to improve focus, start by modifying your work environment. Make sure that the spot you are working in is comfortable. Invest money in a really comfortable and ergonomic office chair. Putting pictures up particularly those with landscapes or other natural images can help improve focus and the overall feel of the environment. Also, find a way to reduce as many distractions as possible. Close your door, close your e-mail, and silence your text alerts. Listening to instrumental music may help or using a white noise machine that masks other noises.

Nutrition is another key to concentration. Make sure to drink plenty of water, if we don't have enough fluid in our body, our muscles and organs (including our brains) do not function at their prime. Eating a breakfast with a combination of complex carbohydrates and protein can help to reduce distractions from hunger and help your body function at its peak. In related news- make sure you get up and move about during the day.

These other ideas may also help your mind to focus:

- Set aside time to deal with worries so you can concentrate on the task at hand while knowing you can address your worries later
- Focus on one task at a time- avoid multitasking
- Switch between tasks that require a lot of attention and those that do not throughout the day
- Prioritize
- Take short breaks
- Do your hardest tasks first if that is when you are alert and fresh
- Reward yourself (chocolate anyone?)

Chapter 12: Multitasking

There are those who claim that one of their greatest skills is multitasking. They are proud of it. They will be saddened to know that multiple studies have shown multitasking to be highly ineffective in becoming more productive and efficient. In fact, some studies report that multitasking can reduce productivity by as much as 40%. Multitasking does not usually refer to two things that are being done simultaneously but rather, the process of switching back and forth between tasks rapidly. When we continually switch tasks, our brain has more difficulty focusing on what is important and ignoring distractions. Eventually, all of this information and switching can cause a "mental bottleneck" that significantly slows down our progress.

A study conducted at the University of Michigan showed that participants who multitasked suffered from a loss of productivity of about 20-40%.

The first step in the task switching process is "stimulus identification". We are interrupted or distracted and interpret that stimulus within the current context. Then "goal shifting" occurs. This is the process of deciding to do one thing instead of another. Next, our goals change through "response selection" based on that new stimulus. Then "role activation" occurs and our brain changes the rules from the previous task to the rules for the new task. The next step in task switching is "movement production" where you begin acting on the steps towards reaching the new goal. This process takes at least half a second. As more multitasking occurs, the time for this process to complete grows.

Our ability to switch tasks depends on many things including our perception, task complexity, task importance, task familiarity, attention span, and our own cognition. Multitasking while completing tasks that are relatively simple or routine - is much easier than switching between two highly complex activities. If both tasks are highly important, more attention and focus is required to complete each with care.

People who multitask tend to make more mistakes than do people who are focused on a single task. Completing two tasks at the same time can be dangerous, as in the case of people who drive and text at the same time. Our brains are simply not made to focus attention on multiple activities at the same time. That said, multitasking can make people feel more energized, engaged, and efficient with multitasking. Multitasking frequently or for a long period on time will put us into a state of stress and we begin demonstrating all the negative effects of that state as well.

There are some alternatives to multitasking that are more efficient and will give help those with short attention spans or bore easily to remain engaged. Firstly, try serial tasking. Switch off between different tasks every 15 minutes or so. For example, make a 15 minute phone call and then write a business plan for 15 minutes, and then check your e-mail. If restlessness still sets in, alternate thinking tasks with body tasks where you can get moving.

Chapter 13: Delegating

Not all tasks that you come across need to be completed by you. They can be delegated to a spouse, daughter, son, co-worker, committee member etc. When you assign activities to others, you can focus on tasks that require your skill set and thus achieve a common goal more quickly. Delegating requires that you know your own strengths and limitations. Pass down those tasks that push the boundaries of your knowledge or capabilities, particularly if you know of others who have more skill completing it.

Delegating begins by choosing a person to complete the task. It is important to find someone who is highly qualified or who has strengths in key areas that would help them to complete the assignment. Also, delegate to someone that makes you feel comfortable and who you enjoy working closely with already. One of the keys to effective delegating is communication and it is much easier to communicate and give feedback to people we are comfortable with and have respect for.

After choosing a qualified person, it is time to clearly present that task to them. Keep in mind that delegating involves asking someone to complete a task; it does not tell them how to complete the task. In order to complete a task, the person needs to be given clear expectations for task completion as well as a well-defined description of what the end result should be. Research has shown that 7 weeks per year are lost by workers needing to seek out clarification due to poor initial communication. Give comprehensive, clear, simple, and concise instructions. Also provide the person with a reasonable but definitive deadline. If it is a large or lengthy assignment, you may consider establishing milestones that will allow you to assess how the project is going and provide feedback as necessary.

Throughout the period of time the person is completing the task you assigned them, make yourself available to answer his or her questions. It may help to establish how the person should go about contacting you at the same time the project is assigned.   For example, if you would prefer to be e-mailed versus telephoned, make that clear.   It is also important to provide routine feedback.   Also, do not forget to thank the person who is assisting you with the project.

Some people have difficulty delegating because it does involve relinquishing some control.   Delegating is risky in some respects due to that reduced control.   However, if done correctly it can be an invaluable tool not only to free you up for other tasks but also to give others the opportunity to learn and apply their knowledge.   You must inhibit any desire to take the task back because you feel you can do it better or faster.   Instead, set up feedback sessions at a frequency that you feel comfortable with so you can help to guide the person you delegated the task to towards completing it successfully.   It is acceptable, and often times helpful, to set limits and suggestions without directing the entire task.

Chapter 14: Procrastination

"Procrastination is the thief of time" - Edward Young Night Thoughts, 1742

Procrastination is a major cause of poor time management.   Psychologists believe that procrastination is not a problem with a person's ability to manage time but more a demonstration of a maladaptive thought process.   People who procrastinate frequently lie to themselves.   For example he or she may say "I don't feel like doing this know but I know I will enjoy doing it tomorrow" they also sometimes fool themselves into thinking certain tasks are not important.   Distractions are a procrastinator's best friend and they frequently seek them out.

People procrastinate for a variety of reasons and in order to tackle it head on, the reason must be identified.   You may procrastinate for a variety of reasons including:

- a task is too overwhelming
- routine has made a person feel restless

- fear of failure
- self-doubt
- fear of stepping out of one's comfort zone
- habit
- poor job value
- urgency
- temptation of distracters

Joseph Ferrari, Ph.D., associate professor of psychology at De Paul University states that there are 3 types of procrastinators. First, there are those people who seek a thrill or adrenaline surge. These people complete tasks at the last minute in order to feel the adrenaline rush course through their systems. On the other hand, there are the avoiders who have a fear of failure, or even a fear of success. Because these people are concerned about how they are perceived by others, they prefer to be seen as someone who does not put in adequate effort versus someone who does not have adequate ability. The last type of procrastinator is the person who cannot make a decision. By not making these decisions, they free themselves from the responsibility that arises based on the outcome of a task.

People frequently talk about procrastination as if it is a trait they were genetically cursed with. Well that is simply not true, procrastination can be defeated and should not be viewed as simply a personality trait that we cannot change or alter. Being a procrastinator is not part of anybody's true nature. That said-procrastination is not easy to overcome, it does take some work. Let us take a look at some strategies to apply in order to stop procrastination.

A study completed by Piers Steel was published in the Psychological Bulletin in 2007. His research showed that procrastination makes people less wealthy, less healthy, and less happy. According to Steel, procrastination is on the rise. In 1978, 5% of American's thought of themselves as procrastinators. This skyrocketed to 26% by 2007. He found that 55 out of every 100 self-identified procrastinators were male.

The most important strategy is to spend less time thinking and planning and spend more time doing. Ruminating over a challenging task is pretty common. There may be a tendency to spend a lot of time thinking about how the project is going to go and how we are going to start it. However, there is also that part of us deep down that finds the whole thing overwhelming and makes us question our capabilities. This fear of failure is a major contributor to procrastination. So we are going to simply stop thinking of all the alternatives and what could go wrong, and simply make a decision - any decision. It is OK if it's the wrong one. Once the task is started, the plan can be revised if it is shown not to work.

One way to stop procrastinating and dive in is to break the task down into more manageable tasks. Once the task has been broken down, take them one step at a time. In that way, you aren't avoiding the whole task, just starting one piece at a time. You'll find that once you get started, you'll feel so much better you'll just keep going. If the job is so overwhelming that breaking it down into smaller pieces still seems like too much, check and make sure the goal and expectations for the task are reasonable. You may find they are not and you will want to address that as needed.

Starting a challenging task early in the day can be beneficial, while you are fresh with the clearest mental clarity. It should be easy to figure out which task will be because it's either the one you are avoiding doing or the one at the top of your nifty prioritized to-do list.

If you just feel like you can't sit and complete the whole task then set a timer for 10 minutes. Work very diligently during that time period. When the 10 minutes is over and you have accomplished something, you will feel a sense of satisfaction, and likely the energy to complete the task.

Reduce distractions. During this time, reduce distractions by stopping your cell phone from ringing and alerting you to texts and e-mails. Close your facebook, twitter, and e-mail windows on your computer.

Plan a day in which to accomplish tasks you have been neglecting. Tie up the loose ends and start fresh.

Tell others about your goals and the tasks you hope to get accomplished. This will help you to be more accountable not just to yourself, but to that friend or family member that is going to ask you what you did later on in the day.

Chapter 15: Eliminating time wasters

Many activities that we complete, sometimes repetitively, on a daily basis result in loss of time and impact our efficiency. Some of these time wasters will be there no matter what we do. However, there are many that we have control over. Even if a time wasting activity cannot be eliminated, it is quite possible to manipulate it in a way to increase efficiency. OfficeTime.net conducted a survey of working professionals in which participants were asked to name their top-3 on-the-job time wasters. 47% of respondents reported that Email was the top time waster. This was followed by procrastination at 42%. Other top time wasters include:

- Social networking 36%
- Meetings 34%
- Surfing the web 30%
- Personal conversations while on the clock 24%
- Repairing technical issues (i.e. computer) 23%
- Fighting "red tape" 19%
- Commuting time 14%
- Computer games 10%

Time wasters can be broken down into 2 categories, self-imposed time wasters which are things you do to yourself and system-imposed time wasters which someone else is doing to you.   Examples of self-imposed time wasters are:

- visiting with friends
- chatting on the phone
- listening to music
- watching TV
- computer games
- video games
- e-mail
- texting
- daydreaming
- not saying 'no'
- alcohol consumption
- recreational drug use
- not following directions
- making mistakes due to carelessness
- poor study skills
- poor concentration
- lack of planning

System-imposed time wasters include:

- over-extended visits
- phone interruptions
- music from a nearby area
- noise from somewhere nearby
- waiting for others
- unclear assignments or tasks
- too many demands
- solving other people's problems
- mechanical break-downs
- illness
- lack of supervision or instruction
- emergencies
- family obligations
- meetings

Let's look in a bit more detail about how to eliminate, or at least decrease the number of time wasters in our day.

In our society where we are always linked in social media via voice calls, texts, Facebook, twitter, Skype etc., we are constantly being distracted by alerts from these types of communication. Pulling yourself away from the task in order to immediately attend to these things costs time. Instead, you could devote a certain amount of time per day or hour to respond to e-mails, texts, check Facebook statuses, etc. Using voicemail to screen calls is a great way to prioritize your workload and respond to only to things that are important and/or urgent.

Having a schedule with small gaps of time between meetings or activities can also waste time if you have not pre-planned tasks that could be accomplished in the bits of time between appointments. If you cannot eliminate these brief periods of time, be sure to have a reading material or other small, tasks that can be easily ended when it is time for your next scheduled activity.

Everybody needs a break. Set a goal to focus on a task for a specific period of time, say one hour, and then allow yourself to take a 10-15 minute break. Use this time to watch TV, play a video game, chat on the phone, or respond to text messages. If you need to, set a timer to alert you when break time is over and it is time to return to work. Simply by knowing that you will have time to engage in some less challenging, fun activities, you will be able to focus more intently on the task at hand.

Constantly functioning in crisis mode is also a time waster. This forces people to be problem focused and working to repair things that are already broken versus being solution focused so things do not break down in the first place. Just like with a car, in many aspects of life maintenance is a lot more costly than repairs.

A significant amount of time can be lost when there is a lack of information, cooperation and/or poor management. One of the biggest wastes of time is meetings that seem to have no agenda or purpose.   For a meeting to be effective, it must have a clearly stated goal or purpose, take a minimum amount of time, and leave people feeling like the meeting had a planned progression towards an end-point.   There are several ways to get meetings started promptly including:

- Clearly stating, preferably in writing, the time at which the meeting is to begin
- Start the meeting at the set time regardless of who is there.   No more, "We will give so-and-so a couple more minutes to get here".   Not only is that not fair to the people who arrived on time, if people realize that you are not going to wait for them, they will likely make more of an effort to arrive on time.
- Before you set a meeting time, ask key attendees what time would be best for them.   Particularly if you find certain people are consistently late, ask for their input as to what time would be more appropriate
- When scheduling meetings, let attendees know how long it will last and keep it short.   People are less likely to be late for a 15 minute meeting than they are to a 60 minute meeting.
- Reward people who arrive on time.   Perhaps bringing a tasty treat that disappears 5 minutes after the meeting's start time so people who are late are not permitted to indulge.   Food is a huge motivator! Giving out a small gift card to a coffee shop or local store to the first person to arrive may be effective as well.
- Invite only people who are vital to achieving the meeting's objective.   The more chefs in the kitchen, the more difficult it will be to start and run an efficient meeting.
- Set a consequence for the last person to arrive.   For example, maybe the last person to arrive needs to

clean up the room after the meeting or is responsible for typing up meeting notes.

Not only is starting meetings on time important, ending them on time is equally as important. Here are some strategies for ending meeting in a timely fashion:

- Clearly set and state a time for ending the meeting. If the objectives of the meeting have not been achieved by that time, schedule a follow-up meeting.
- Use a visual countdown timer that all can see during the meeting.
- If the objective of the meeting is met before the set ending time, leave early. No sense dragging it out.
- Allow people to leave when they need to. Some people may not need to provide input or information after a certain point. It is advantageous to all for them to be permitted to leave and engage in other, more productive, tasks.
- Set an alarm to ring when the end time has been reached.
- Use an agenda complete with time marked milestones.
- When time is up, require everybody to stand up. They can keep talking but you will find that people will not waste time if they are not permitted to sit. In fact, if you want to keep an entire meeting short, make it a standing meeting.
- After the allotted time is passed, you can simply excuse yourself. Stand up, state "I have another meeting" and leave. Done.

Other common work-related wasters include:

- Making decisions without data
- Unsure of responsibilities
- Lack of goals/planning
- Red tape
- Too much paperwork

- Poor filing system
- Inadequate resources
- Untrained staff
- Under staffed
- Lack of cooperation
- Interruptions from management
- Continuous meetings
- Incomplete information
- Poor self-discipline
- Too many tasks
- No standards of performance
- Poor communication
- Other people on a team are not working effectively
- Unnecessary communications
- Poor instructions
- Lack of management decisions
- Customer demands

Chapter 16: Why, when, and how to say NO

Learning to say "no" is a great way to reduce interruptions in your day. When someone asks someone to do something they do not want to do they tend to either:

- Give in and say "yes" when we really want to say "no"
- Say "no" in an ineffective way
- Say nothing at all and hope the person goes away and doesn't ask again

People have difficulty saying "no" for a variety of reasons. Firstly, many people really want to help others and we find it hard to put our goals first in order to do that. Others feel that by saying "no" they are being rude. Still others have a strong desire to be agreeable and avoid conflict. There is also the fear of losing opportunities and burning bridges by declining someone's request, particularly if they are higher up the ladder than you. In order to say 'no' and feel alright about it, you must know that you truly do not have the time to complete the request. This is done by having clearly defined goals for how your time is being spent. Once you have a goal, you can evaluate requests and decide if you have time to participate, if it will help you accomplish your goals, or if you want to do it.   After this period of evaluation, either accept the request, or reject it, in a prompt manner.   By not responding quickly, you are likely to spend more time dealing with the request as it will be brought to your attention again in the future.

There are several reasons why we should say 'no' to someone for their own good.   By saying 'no' to someone because we are not highly qualified to complete a task, we are allowing the asker to find someone who has a greater ability to complete the task and do it well.   If you say 'yes' when you really do not want the task, you will harbor some bad feelings towards that person for asking you to do it which, could in turn negatively affect your relationship with him or her.

Saying 'no' can be very challenging but try to feel a sense of satisfaction for achieving your goals instead of feeling guilty by not accepting the request of another.   Try one of these ways:

- "I'm sorry but I can't do that right now"
- "I can't commit to this as I have other things on my plate at this time"
- "I'm not comfortable with that"
- "I'm not taking on any new responsibilities right now"
- "Let me think about it and get back to you" (reminder-   it will take another interaction and time later to clear this up)
- "I need to leave some time for myself right now"
- "I would rather help with another duty"
- "I'm in the middle of something right now.   What don't we touch base at X o'clock and talk about it briefly?"
- "My calendar is full, I don't think I can fit another thing on it"
- "I have another commitment"

- "Sounds interesting but I have not experience with that so I'll have to decline"
- "Thanks for thinking of me but I know you will be wonderful at that yourself"
- "This doesn't meet my needs right now but I'll be sure to keep you in mind"
- "I'm not sure I'm the best person to assist you with this.   Why don't you try talking with ___?"
- "No, I can't."
- "I can't do this, but I can ….."

Try to be firm, polite, and sympathetic.   Avoid being overly apologetic and avoid providing a detailed explanation as to why you can't help them out.   You do not owe them that, he or she should recognize that everyone has a lot of work and limited time to accomplish it in.

Chapter 17: Using technology to your advantage

Lap top computers

One of the most important pieces of technology to assist with time management is a laptop computer.   They are primarily beneficial because they are portable and able to use during 'down times'.   If you are waiting for a meeting to start, pull out your computer and whip out an e-mail or type up some notes.   Make sure that you have a program that will synchronize documents between your desktop, laptop, and Smartphone if you are using multiple machines.

Tablets

The iPad and other tablets have some great tools to increase productivity and efficiency.   These features include:

- Large screen size
- Multitouch interface

- Internet connectivity
- Visible to-do list
- Large, easy-to-use calendar
- Document library
- Note taking ease
- Portability

E-mail

If you receive a lot of e-mails each day, you will easily recognize that it is not easy to keep track of them and organize them in a helpful manner. In order to increase efficiency in this area, checking multiple e -mails at set times each day can be helpful. For example, check it first thing in the morning, after lunch, and shortly before leaving. If you frequently find yourself distracted by knowing you have an e-mail and are unable to resist interrupting your work to check it, try changing the settings on your e-mail software to only check the server and download e-mails at certain times. Checking e-mail is also a way to build in a short break between longer, more challenging tasks. When you do check your e-mail, try to apply the 2-minute rule. Open the e-mail. If it can be read and responded to in less than 2-minutes, go ahead and do so, even if it is not particularly important or urgent. This saves more time than locating the file and re-reading it later. For e-mails that will take longer than 2-minutes, add it to your action or to-do list. Use your e-mail program to highlight or flag the message for easy access later.

As with paper and electronic documents, e-mails must also be filed in an accurate and efficient manner. Start by creating folders by categories. You can use broad categories such as, "waiting for response", "reference", "action", and "archives" or you can use narrower categories such as "clients", "family", "bills", etc. depending on your needs.

Software

Some people choose to use their android, tablet, iphone or ipad to manage their lives. Many, many apps are available to assist with task management and in particular, creating project, to-do, or action lists. Task manager applications generally let you input your tasks into different categories: projects, lists, appointments etc. Many take that information to create to-do or action lists. The first style of app takes an action list approach. This involves using a single list that contains a particular day's tasks, frequently integrated with a calendar, along with any you may add manually. These apps usually allow the user to easily add or remove tasks from the list, move tasks to and from another list, and add tasks with a due date of "today" to the action list. This style gives the user complete control of what is on the list. This is also the disadvantage as time must be invested into adding, deleting, and prioritizing the list's items. Other applications apply general 'rules' to determine tasks you are currently working on and create a list. This has the advantage of being created with little direct work from you. However, you lose control over your tasks and ability to add, delete, and prioritize. Some software programs use a set of lists that each serves a particular purpose. For example, lists may include, "projects due today", "urgent tasks", or "overdue tasks". By looking through multiple lists, the user can determine what to work on. These lists are shorter and give a different perspective to choosing tasks. The disadvantage is it is needed to check several lists to make sure all responsibilities are addressed and nothing gets neglected.

There are many applications that can be used to manage tasks and to-do lists. MindMeister, is one such application. It is cloud-based, meaning it can be accessed from multiple devices. With it, you create a visual representation of your goals rather than relying on lists. Because it exists on a cloud, you can allow others to view, edit, and collaborate with you on a goal. For people who love using lists, List.ly is a great tool. On it, you can create a to-do list but since it is cloud-based others can view it, make modifications, and provide feedback. If you are looking for a simple, portable, electronic to-do list, try to remember the Milk. This application is compatible with Siri on the iPhone 4S.

Other applications help to analyze how your time is being used. One such application is RescueTime. It is downloaded onto a windows or Macintosh computer and records how long you spend using a program or completing an activity as you work. It compiles information and analyzes how you are using your time. This allows you to estimate task time more accurately and become more efficient. Toggl can be used on a Smartphone, Mac, and PC. It saves your entire project and keeps track of the amount of time spent while completing it. For tasks that you do repeatedly, you can try to beat your last times.

There are still other programs that increase productivity in other ways. ActiveWords is a Smartphone application that saves time while inputting information. The user starts by assigning abbreviations to lengthy chunks of information, similar to the autocorrect feature on a phone. For example you could program the application to replace the word "address" with your complete address and additional contact information. A great decision-making application is Grid Analysis. You enter your options into a table and then enter information in a variety of factors into columns. You then score each option and the application then provides you with information on the best decision given the factors you have inputted.

Using an on-line dropbox or cloud can also help to save time. They are especially useful for people who are using any combinations of laptop, home pc, office pc, Smartphone, or tablet. With a dropbox or cloud, you will know where the most recently updated version of a file is, no matter where you are accessing it. The process of e-mailing files to yourself is eliminated. This saves time in sending as well as retrieving on the other end. Clouds are a great way to store reference files that you need handy wherever you go. All of your work can be set up to be automatically synced to the cloud. If you don't want it to be automatic it can be as simple as dragging and dropping a file. You also do not need to worry about losing a USB stick or other portable media format. Clouds and dropboxes also have the advantage of allowing others to view your files for collaborative and revision purposes. If you don't want others to have direct access, you can quickly share a single file via e-mail directly from the cloud.

Chapter 18: Motivations to manage your time

Staying motivated to accomplish your time management goals can be a challenge. At times, it will seem like you are not making any progress. The biggest piece of advice is to keep going. Do not give up. It will get easier. Try some of these tools during those times when you feel like abandoning your journey to higher efficiency.

Start by reflecting and reviewing your goals and priorities. If your goals were made in the way suggested early, they will be trackable so your progress should be apparent once you look at the data. Once you notice your accomplishments, write them in a journal that you can turn to in moments of despair and desperation. Also, tell others about your accomplishments. Show-off and brag a little, work towards the top of Maslow's hierarchy!

Now this next suggestion seems to be used as a cure-all for everything. And for good reason- it can cure all, or most, issues and ailments. The suggestion is exercise. Using energy breeds energy. Once you get moving, it is easy to keep going. Not only will your body become healthier, your mind will be sharper and can focus and concentrate much better. Exercise results in increased adrenaline. After exercising you will have more energy. Being physically fit and active boosts your confidence. When confidence is boosted in one area, confidence increases in others as well. Exercise can also increase your capacity to get more done, inspire creative ideas, and build momentum for challenging projects. If you think you do not have time to exercise, make it! Build it into your day as a priority. You may find you are more successful with fitting it in if you do it early in the day. Try squeezing in small workouts. You do not need a gym. Go for a walk, do push-ups, sit-ups, use a fitness DVD or software program.

Reading motivational quotes and/or articles may also give you the boost you need to keep on trucking. Here is a couple to get you started:

- *"Don't say you don't have enough time. You have exactly the same number of hours per day that were given to Helen Keller, Pasteur, Michelangelo, Mother Teresa, Leonardo da Vinci, Thomas Jefferson, and Albert Einstein." -- H. Jackson Brown*
- *"The bad news is time flies. The good news is you're the pilot." -- Michael Altshuler*
- *"A wise person does at once, what a fool does at last. Both do the same thing; only at different times." -- Baltasar Gracian*
- *"To think too long about doing a thing often becomes its undoing." -- Eva Young*
- *"A year from now you will wish you had started today." -- Karen Lamb*
- *"The surest way to be late is to have plenty of time." -- Leo Kennedy*

Starting something that you have been putting off is a great way to get motivated. Do not set out with the goal of finishing a task, simply start it. By taking this first step, many people find that they naturally develop the energy to continue. Energy breeds energy. On the other hand, instead of starting a new task, you could work on finishing a task that you have already started. These strategies also have the advantage of building confidence and a sense of self-satisfaction that can have an even greater benefit than increased productivity.

Many people are inspired by music. If you are one of those people, play a song that has the effect of getting you up, moving, and feeling more energetic- dance or sing-along if you need to. Once you get this energy surge, you will feel more alert and able to continue, or start, a project.

Cleaning up or changing environments gives the sense of making a fresh start. Humans are visually oriented, and working in an unclean or cluttered space can make us feel less energetic and focused. By tidying up, or moving to another spot, we feel like we can begin again from a blank slate.

Use other people to motivate you. Talk to someone about your goals for the day or the week. The person is likely to ask you about it later and we have a tendency to care about what other people think. Therefore, we may be more productive as a result of wanting to be able to report success.

Giving yourself a small external reward for small accomplishments can go a long way. Is there a special food treat you would like? A movie you would like to see? Do you want a manicure? These small enticements just might be enough to spark you into action.

People often use visualization tools for maintaining momentum during the goal achievement process. To start the visualization process, ask yourself the following questions and write down your responses, in detail. Try to create a picture of your answers in your writing.

- When I have achieved my goal, what will I see?
- What will I look like when I have achieved my goal?
- What will I have when my goal has been achieved?
- How will I celebrate my achievement?
- What will other people see when I have achieved my goal?

You may want to find or create images that depict this and create a collage or post them on your bulletin board. Make it highly visible in an environment you frequent.

Chapter 19: Tools for time management

Throughout this report you have been presented with several tools to increase your productivity and efficiency. These have included planners, organizers, PDA's, Smartphones, and mobile applications. In this chapter you will find even more tools that may assist you with time management.

Planners and organizers:

- **Moleskin Academic Weekly Pocket Notebook**

    ❖ Hardcover with ribbon bookmark and elastic closure
    ❖ Expandable inner pocket
    ❖ Address book
    ❖ Weekly view
    ❖ Plenty of lined note pages
    ❖ Cost is $12.89 on Amazon

- **House of Doolittle academic Weekly Planner**

    ❖ 5x8 inches made of recycled materials
    ❖ One week view on a two page spread
    ❖ Monthly planning section
    ❖ Metric to English conversion table
    ❖ List of common formulas
    ❖ Project record space
    ❖ Cost is $9.24 on Amazon

- **At-A-Glance Recycled Weekly Appointment Book**

    ❖ 8 ¼ by 10 inches
    ❖ Quarter-hourly appointments from 7 am to 8:45 pm
    ❖ Once week view on a two page spread
    ❖ Telephone and address pages
    ❖ Cost is $15.99 on Amazon

- **At-A-Glance Standard Diary**

  - ❖ 5 by 8 inches
  - ❖ Hardcover
  - ❖ One day per page
  - ❖ Telephone and address pages
  - ❖ Month expense summary section
  - ❖ Cost is $13.85 on Amazon

- **Moleskine Ruled Notebook**

  - ❖ Bookmark and elastic closure
  - ❖ Expandable inner pocket
  - ❖ Durable
  - ❖ Journal format
  - ❖ Cost is $12.21 on Amazon

- **DayMinder Premiere Recycled Monthly Planner**

  - ❖ 8 by 11 inches
  - ❖ One month per two page spread
  - ❖ Hardcover with concealed wire
  - ❖ Storage pocket
  - ❖ Monthly tabs
  - ❖ Cost is $11.90 on Amazon

Software and applications:

- **Launchy**

  - ❖ Windows-based
  - ❖ Launches files, folders, and programs with one keystroke instead of searching on desktop, the start menu, or file manager.
  - ❖ Free

- **Quicksilver**

  - ❖ Mac-based

- ❖ Launches files, folders, and programs with one keystroke instead of searching on desktop, the start menu, or file manager.
- ❖ Assists with tasks such as running scripts and sending e-mail
- ❖ Free

- **Google Calendar**

  - ❖ Create schedules
  - ❖ Reminders of important dates
  - ❖ Can by synchronized and accessed across multiple devices
  - ❖ Free

- **WakeupOnStandy**

  - ❖ Windows-based
  - ❖ Wakes the computer up from stand-by mode and automatically performs tasks such as running a program or checking e-mail
  - ❖ Free

- **NowDoThis**

  - ❖ Mobile application
  - ❖ Simple, quick to-do list
  - ❖ Free

- **Checkvist**

  - ❖ Web-based with mobile versions
  - ❖ Task list allowing for hierarchical lists
  - ❖ Allows for sharing and collaboration
  - ❖ Note-taking ability
  - ❖ E-mail notifications
  - ❖ Reminders
  - ❖ Free for basic account

- **Lastpass**

  - ❖ PC, Mac, Web, and mobile access
  - ❖ Stores passwords
  - ❖ Fills in on-line forms quickly
  - ❖ Free

- **Mind42**

  - ❖ Web-based
  - ❖ Visually organizes tasks that need to be completed
  - ❖ Free

- **Syncback Freeware**

  - ❖ PC, Mac,   Smartphone, Web accessible
  - ❖ Backs-up and syncs information automatically
  - ❖ Free

- **Workrave**

  - ❖ Windows and GNU/Linux compatible
  - ❖ Alerts you to take breaks during tasks
  - ❖ Restricts you to a limit on the number of breaks you take
  - ❖ Free

- **101 Smart Goals**

  - ❖ Web-based
  - ❖ Create and manage your goals
  - ❖ 3-step process to goal achievement
  - ❖ Free

- **Basecamp**

  - ❖ Web-based
  - ❖ Easy to create and manage to-do lists

- Time-tracking feature captures how much time is spend on a particular task
- Free

- **Evernote**

  - Windows, Mac, Web, and Mobile formats
  - Collect notes in one place
  - Clip web pages, files, and much more
  - Create a document instantly
  - Free

- **Mozy**

  - Window and Mac formats
  - Backs up files including documents, pictures, and video onto a cloud automatically
  - Free

Books:

- **The 7 Habits of Highly Effective People by Stephen Covey**

  - Published November 2004
  - Description from Amazon- *"In The 7 Habits of Highly Effective People, author Stephen R. Covey presents a holistic, integrated, principle-centered approach for solving personal and professional problems. With penetrating insights and pointed anecdotes, Covey reveals a step-by-step pathway for living with fairness, integrity, service, and human dignity--principles that give us the security to adapt to change and the wisdom and power to take advantage of the opportunities that change creates."*

- **Time Management from the Inside Out by Julie Morgenstern**

- ❖ Published September 2000
- ❖ Description from Amazon- *"America's #1 organizer now takes on our biggest enemy--the time crunch In this fast-moving world, no greater challenge exists--in both our personal and professional lives--than organizing and managing our time. Now Julie Morgenstern, whose bestselling book, Organizing from the Inside Out, has become the new standard in this category, explains how to meet and conquer the time challenge once and for all. Morgenstern's groundbreaking "from-the-inside-out" approach helps readers uncover their own psychological stumbling blocks and strengths, and develop a time-management system that suits their individual needs. By applying her proven three-step program--analyze, strategize, and attack--and following her effective guidelines, readers will find more time for work, family, self-improvement, or whatever is most important to them. As Francis Willet, founder and CFO of Day Runner, says, "Morgenstern shows us how to look inside at our own habits and style to create a plan that works, and have fun doing it."*

- **Juggling Elephants by James Loflin and Todd Musig**

  - ❖ Published September 2007
  - ❖ Description from Amazon- *"What do you do when your life feels as busy as a three-ring circus? Juggling Elephants tells a simple but profound story about one man with a universal problem. Mark has too much to do, too many priorities, too much stress, and too little time. As he struggles to balance his many responsibilities without cracking under the pressure, Mark takes a break to attend the circus with his family. There he has a surprising conversation with a wise ringmaster. He leaves with a simple but powerful lesson: Trying to get everything done is like juggling elephants -- impossible. So Mark begins to think about his work, family, and personal life the way a ringmaster thinks about the many acts in a three-ring*

circus. He discovers that managing his various acts can be fun and easy once he changes his attitude and follows his new friend's ongoing guidance. Mark soon realizes:
* If you keep trying to juggle elephants, no one, including you, will be thrilled with your performance.
* A ringmaster cannot be in all three rings at once.
* The key to the success of a circus is having quality acts in all three rings.
* Intermission is an essential part of any good circus.
Juggling Elephants is a wonderfully lighthearted guide for everyone who feels like they're about to be squashed. It will help you better focus your time and energy, so you'll be able to enjoy more of the things that are important to you. Above all, it will teach you how to run your circus, instead of letting the circus run you.

- **Thriving 24/7 by Sally Helgesen**

  ❖ Published July 2001
  ❖ *Description* from Amazon-" *Thriving in 24/7 is a guide to navigating a new world of work in which all the rules have changed. In the 24/7 world, home can seem like a branch office. E-mail beckons at 3 A.M.; we work not nine-to-five but across multiple time zones; beeper messages interrupt private moments. Whether we're planning a vacation, choosing health insurance, or buying a car, we are flooded with so many options that our personal lives feel like second jobs. Even the pleasures that should refresh us -- Thanksgiving dinner or lunch with a close friend -- too often seem like tasks on an infinite to-do list. How, asks Sally Helgesen, do we keep from being swallowed up by a world that is fundamentally out of sync with human nature? Helgesen, a premier thinker on the role of work in the knowledge economy, offers readers six powerful strategies for achieving and maintaining equilibrium in this new world. Drawing upon dozens of interviews with men and women adept at navigating life in 24/7, she urges us to:*
  START AT THE CORE: We can move more nimbly

in a complex world if we confront personal history, locate our inner voice, get comfortable in the neutral zone, and take inventory on a regular basis. LEARN TO ZIGZAG: We can master the art of improvisation if we learn from the youngest generation, think in terms of "gigs," plan to keep learning all our lives, rework our definitions of loyalty, and internalize optimism. CREATE OUR OWN WORK: We can do this (even if we stay in our present jobs) by articulating our value, integrating our passions, identifying our market, running our own shop, and targeting multiple centers of gravity. WEAVE A STRONG WEB OF INCLUSION: We can build the support we need if we learn to go deep fast, understand the strength of weak ties, grab the spotlight, and master the simple art of looking people up. BUILD A CLEAR BRAND: We can brand ourselves unforgettably by becoming highly conscious of our practice, our materials, our design, and the symbols that we use. PRACTICE THE RHYTHM OF RENEWAL: We can find true refreshment if we learn to connect with timeless rhythms, identify the true sources of our joy, practice mindfulness, and cultivate the elements of Slow. Writing with simple eloquence and piercing intelligence, Sally Helgesen shows us that bucking up or burning out aren't the only choices if we want to get ahead. This indispensable handbook offers an imaginative, sometimes radical, blueprint for achieving balance in an unbalanced world.

- **REWORK by Jason Friedman and David Heinemeier Hansson**

  ❖ Published March 2010
  ❖ Description from Amazon- *"Most business books give you the same old advice: Write a business plan, study the competition, seek investors, yadda yadda. If you're looking for a book like that, put this one back on the shelf. Rework shows you a better, faster, easier way to succeed in business. Read it and you'll know why plans are actually*

harmful, why you don't need outside investors, and why you're better off ignoring the competition. The truth is, you need less than you think. You don't need to be a workaholic. You don't need to staff up. You don't need to waste time on paperwork or meetings. You don't even need an office. Those are all just excuses. What you really need to do is stop talking and start working. This book shows you the way. You'll learn how to be more productive, how to get exposure without breaking the bank, and tons more counterintuitive ideas that will inspire and provoke you. With its straightforward language and easy-is-better approach, Rework is the perfect playbook for anyone who's ever dreamed of doing it on their own. Hardcore entrepreneurs, small-business owners, people stuck in day jobs they hate, victims of "downsizing," and artists who don't want to starve anymore will all find valuable guidance in these pages"

- **Mindmapping by Joyce Wycoff**

  ❖ *Published* June 1991
  ❖ *Description* from Amazon- *"Readers can finally break down the blocks that hinder free thinking and discover their vast stores of innovative ideas involving whole-brain thinking techniques presented here. "A no-nonsense, practical guide to help put creative powers to work!"--Michael LeBoeuf, author of Imagineering."*

PowerPoint Presentations

- **Balancing Time and Commitments**

  ❖ *http://www.effective-time-management-strategies. com/media-files/balancing_time_and_commitme nts.ppt*

- **Getting Things Done by David Allen ET. al**

❖ http://www.effective-time-management-strategies
.com/media-files/gtd.ppt

Papers and articles

- *"Time Management"* by Columbus Citywide Training
  and Development Center
- *"***Time*** *Management:* *A New Approach from Ancient
  Greece!"* by Eric Garner

Other tools

- **Pen and paper**
- **Wall calendar**
- **White board**
- **Dry erase calendar**
- **Bulletin board**
- **In-box**
- **Paper shredder**

Websites

- www.mindtools.com
- www.stevepavlina.com
- www.time-management-coach.com
- http://www.time-management-guide.com
- http://www.psychologytoday.com
- http://www.markforster.net/
- www.usingmindmaps.com

9232044R00051

Printed in Great Britain
by Amazon.co.uk, Ltd.,
Marston Gate.